ADVANCE PRAISE FOR

We Be Lovin' Black Children:
Learning to Be Literate About the African Diaspora

The title, *We Be Lovin' Black Children*, establishes its premise. 'Be Lovin' connotes an immediacy, a now-ness, a persistence that is culturally based and applicable to today's enigmatic conditions. Give every new African and African American mother a copy of *We Be Lovin' Black Children* and the intricate, complex maze through which she must meander in her quest for emotional freedom is diminished. *We Be Lovin' Black Children* means we have been, are now, and will be lovin' and minimizing the barriers that separate us. It is explicit and replete with examples of the *how*. With the wisdom of loving scholars and teachers, the chains of oppression are weakened and eventually severed.

Dr. Adelaide L. Sanford, Vice-Chancellor Emerita, New York State Board of Regents

Black parents can no longer settle for 'the Talk' as a defense for our children. They need information, strategies, and tactics for ensuring Black children survive AND thrive in an increasingly hostile world. *We Be Lovin' Black Children* is the corrective our families need to raise the mentally, emotionally, socially, and culturally healthy children we need to ensure the legacies left over the millennia and throughout the world.

Dr. Gloria Ladson-Billings
Professor Emerita and the former Kellner Family Distinguished Professor at the University of Wisconsin-Madison, past President of the American Educational Research Association (AERA)

As educational systems consistently demonstrate anti-Blackness through their policies and practices, this book shows readers what it means to be pro-Black and consequently pro-Black children. By tearing down divisive barriers and unnecessary borders, the book exemplifies what is possible in a global movement dedicated to Blackness in the fight for racial justice! This book teaches as it troubles racial injustices everywhere!

Dr. H. Richard Milner IV
Cornelius Vanderbilt Chair of Education,
Vanderbilt University

We Be Lovin' Black Children

May 2021

Dear Beulah,

At ABFE's May board meeting, I announced that all new board members would be gifted this book.

It dawned on me that all board members should get it since the purpose is to keep our eyes on the prize.

Thank you for your leadership in service to Black children & their families!

Love,
Debra

We Be Lovin' Black Children

Learning to Be Literate About the African Diaspora

EDITED BY

GLORIA SWINDLER BOUTTE,
JOYCE E. KING,
GEORGE L. JOHNSON, JR.,
AND LAGARRETT J. KING

GORHAM, MAINE

Myers Education Press is an academic publisher specializing in books, e-books, and digital content in the field of education. All of our books are subjected to a rigorous peer review process and produced in compliance with the standards of the Council on Library and Information Resources.

Library of Congress Cataloging-in-Publication Data available from Library of Congress.

13-digit ISBN 978-1-9755-0463-2 (paperback)
13-digit ISBN 978-1-9755-0462-5 (hardcover)
13-digit ISBN 978-1-9755-0464-9 (library networkable e-edition)
13-digit ISBN 978-1-9755-0465-6 (consumer e-edition)

Printed in the United States of America.

All first editions printed on acid-free paper that meets the American National Standards Institute Z39-48 standard.

Books published by Myers Education Press may be purchased at special quantity discount rates for groups, workshops, training organizations, and classroom usage. Please call our customer service department at 1-800-232-0223 for details.

Cover and interior design by Teresa Legrange

Visit us on the web at **www.myersedpress.com** to browse our complete list of titles.

Contents

Acknowledgments

We extend gratitude to our ancestors, family members, friends, and loved ones who made this work possible. Special thanks are extended to the magnificent Dr. (Nana) Joyce E. King, who introduced the concept of diaspora literacy and inspired generations of scholar-activists—some of whom contributed to this work and scores of unnamed mentees and admirers. As usual, Jarvais Jackson, University of South Carolina doctoral student, willingly shared his artistic talents not only to design the conference booklet but also the cover of this book. Thanks to Angela Hill, doctoral student at the University of South Carolina, for her editorial assistance.

This book is the product of a small conference funded by the Spencer Foundation, which focused on African diaspora literacy in September 2019. Thanks to program officers, reviewers, and others who saw the promise in the grant proposal. We hope that this book makes you proud. We acknowledge the following conference attendees and extend deep appreciation for thinking together about how to better love Black children.

Janice Baines	Gloria Swindler Boutte
Anthony Broughton	Michelle Bryan
Saudah Collins	Justus Cox
Julia Dawson	Gwenda Green
Angela Hill	Kayla Hostetler
Joy Howard	Derrick Jackson
Jarvais Jackson	Tambra Jackson
Toby Jenkins	George L. Johnson, Jr.

Joyce E. King

Clement Lambert

Meir Muller

Kindel Nash

Asangha Muki

Nancy Tolson

Kamania Wynter-Hoyte

LaGarrett King

Hassimi Maiga

Susi Long

Mopelola Omoegun

Samuel Ntewesu

Berte Van Wyk

 Preface

Gloria Swindler Boutte, Joyce E. King,
George L. Johnson, Jr., and LaGarrett J. King

W*e be lovin' Black children* is the powerful theme of this book. Authors have strong track records effectively ensuring Black children's cultural and academic excellence. We hail from different U.S. locales and six African diasporic countries. We provide lots of resources.

In Chapter 1, "Open Love Letter to Black Families and Communities," two professors extend an open invitation for Black families to urgently and actively teach children and youth about Black history and contemporary issues.

In Chapter 2, "Say It Loud—I'm Black and I'm Proud: Beauty, Brilliance, and Belonging in Our Homes, Classrooms, and Communities," four outstanding elementary teachers provide examples of activities that can be done with families and community members to ensure that children and youth are culturally grounded.

Written by three exemplary middle school teachers, Chapter 3, "Great Rising: Activities to Inspire Black Teens and Youth," engages readers with insights on "Black Girl Magic," culturally relevant ideas for teaching Black males, and ideas that inspire Black youth.

Chapter 4, "Preparing Black Children to Identify and Confront Racism in Books, Media, and Other Texts: Critical Questions," written by a Jewish professor, emphasizes the power of books and other texts such as music, movies, television, and so forth. Strategies for teaching Black children to critically analyze texts are provided.

Chapter 5, "Each One, Teach One: Reflections and Lessons on Mentoring Young Men of Color," offers mentoring advice for boys (and girls). Everyone is invited to commit to being responsible for the success of Black children and youth. It is written by two professors—one White and one Black.

Chapter 6, "We Are Family," is co-narrated by a White teacher and one of her previous African American students. Together, they demonstrate what welcoming classroom "families" and communities should look like. The student, Jamon, powerfully reflects on the Black love he felt in Mrs. Hostetler's classroom as well as the trauma he felt from the omission of Black history through most of his schooling—other than the poor teaching about slavery and civil rights.

Chapter 7, "The Crown on Your Head: Teaching African Diaspora Literacy Through Hair," is co-authored by an African American elementary teacher and her White university doctoral advisor (who has three Black-mixed sons). Shayla, the teacher, discusses her journey learning to love her natural hair and shares how she teaches the love of Black hair in elementary school.

Chapter 8, "Teaching Our Children About Blackness in the World," is written by three professors. They offer Freedom Schools and elev8te as excellent models for learning about world literacy. Emphasis is on facilitating Black people's critical consciousness around the globe.

Chapter 9, "African Diaspora Literacy in Jamaica and the Wider Caribbean," is written by a professor. It offers an astute analysis of cultural issues regarding color-consciousness as well as insights regarding the influence of European educational systems on Caribbean people.

Chapter 10, "Lessons From Africa," is written by three professors—a Cameroonian, a Ghanaian, and a South African. Readers will learn timeless and generalizable African proverbs, stories, and lessons. These foundational values are essential for the survival of Black children and youth.

Chapter 11, "Resources and Next Steps," written by the four editors, concludes by providing resources and next steps for readers. Emphasis is placed on the urgency of deeply lovin' Black children and youth by helping them become literate about African diasporic history and culture.

Introduction

Gloria Swindler Boutte, Joyce E. King,
George L. Johnson, Jr., and LaGarrett J. King

We Be Lovin' Black Children[1]

Figure A. Adinkra symbol: *Odo nnyew fie kwan,* "love never loses its way home," a symbol of the power of love
Source: http://www.adinkra.org/htmls/adinkra/odon.htm

In the tradition of African culture, we welcome you. This book is *pro*-Black. Pro-Black does not mean *anti*-White or *anti* anything else. It means that this little book is about what we as Black people must do to ensure that Black children across the world are loved and safe and that their souls and spirits are healed from the ongoing damage of living in a world in which White supremacy flourishes. We hope you can endorse that. To be clear, Black children—wherever they are in the world and regardless if they are in majority Black settings or not—need to learn Black history. This book offers insights and tips about how we can make sure that they do. At the time this was written, the world is experiencing the

---

1 During a brainstorming conference at the Conference on African Diaspora Literacy in 2019, Tambra Jackson suggested this title. There was unanimous agreement among the group.

COVID-19 health pandemic, and many children are attending school virtually or via a hybrid learning situation. This book can help support children and parents during this time.

This is a love book (see Figure A for the Adinkra symbol for love), and we want you to read and share it with as many Black people as you can so that collectively we can become literate about our shared culture. We also welcome others to join us in becoming literate in this way. We call this type of literacy, knowledge, and understanding *African diaspora literacy*. This information can literally serve to heal Black people from historical and contemporary trauma that we collectively experience. One thing we know for sure is that no cultural group can survive if they do not know and embrace their history. If you want to learn how to use Black love as a healing salve, then this is the book for you.

Before you put this book down because you think that the language in the title, *We Be Lovin' Black Children*, is not what you expected, let us explain why we chose to use African American Language. African American Language (also called Ebonics, Black English, and other names) is the most distinct dialect in the United States. Despite what you may have heard, it is a highly sophisticated language with distinct features that other dialects do not have. For example, it has five present verb tenses and unique features and uses of words like *be*. That *be* is so powerful that it can mean the past, the present, and the future. Linguists refer to it as the *habitual be*. So when we say that *we **be** lovin' Black children*, it means that we loved them in the *past*, we love them in the *present*, and we will love them in the *future*. No one can make us *not* love them. We love them 24/7—all day, seven days a week; 365/366 days a year. That is deep love, and that is why we wrote this book.

Around the world, there are parallel forms of African American Language—in the United States, Africa, the Caribbean, South America, and so forth. We are proud of this rich language heritage just as we are proud of Black children. The lives and welfare of our children and future generations are in danger if we, as adults, do not help them learn and value their history and understand contemporary issues that affect us all as Black people. The goal of this book is to share the wisdom that we have learned as professors and teachers—and parents. At the same time, we recognize the wisdom among Black people from all walks of life in families, communities, social and political organizations, and educational institutions. Collectively, we can use our love for Black children to make the world a better, safer, and more humane place for them.

How Deep Is Your Love?

The lack of knowledge is darker than the night.

—African Proverb

The preceding African proverb captures what happened to Black people when our ancestors were first brought to the United States and brutally enslaved. White enslavers intentionally and forcefully tried to remove our ancestors' knowledge of anything they knew about their cultures, histories, and identities while brutally exploiting the knowledge and skills that made their labor valuable. The proverb also conveys what has happened to Black people in other places who were colonized by Europeans. This book will help adults and children begin thinking about how to re-member (or put back together) the parts of our heritage that enslavers, laws, mores, and cultural domination intentionally and systematically sought to take from Black people—and still do.

The education of any people should begin with the people themselves, but Negroes thus trained have been dreaming about the ancients of Europe and about those who have tried to imitate them. (Woodson, 1933/1990, p. 32)

This book is intended to be a resource and reference to be consulted often. It contains a wealth of ideas that families, educators, and community members can use to teach Black children and heal them. Please share it widely. Don't be surprised or misled by people who discourage reading the book and engaging Black children in these activities. Remember that there are many people who (1) do not realize that Black children's spirits and psyches are being damaged daily in school and society and (2) do not have Black children's and people's best interest in mind—well-meaning intentions notwithstanding. We hope you will not be deterred by "haters" and that you will do your part to ensure that Black children everywhere know that they are *young, gifted, and Black—and have their souls intact.* This little book could well be the most important book you will ever read.

Finally, we acknowledge the Spencer Foundation's support for the conference on African diaspora literacy in September 2019. This book emerged from a 2-day working conference that convened 30 people, including educational researchers, P–12 classroom teachers, and a community member. Participants were multi-ethnic, multigenerational, international, and multidisciplinary (e.g., from disciplines such as history, social studies, economics, English, African studies, education foundations, early childhood education, secondary education). All attendees were connected via the Center for the Education and Equity of African American Students (www.ceeaas.com). Faculty participants were from historically Black colleges and universities, predominantly White institutions, and international institutions (representing six African diasporic countries—Cameroon, Ghana, Jamaica, Mali, Nigeria, and South Africa). The primary goal was to think together about how to ensure Black people's welfare in the United States and globally. The conference provided a platform for strategizing how best to amplify work on African diaspora literacy and increase its visibility. An important goal was to figure out how to make the scholarship on African diaspora literacy accessible to the wider population beyond educators. This book is an attempt to do so. After you read it, we hope that you will not only feel more informed, but you will also feel a more profound sense of joy about *lovin' Black children and youth*. Happy reading! Stay well.

Part I

BLACK FOLKS IN THE UNITED STATES

1

Kamania Wynter-Hoyte and Gloria Swindler Boutte

Open Love Letter to Black Families and Communities

Dear Black Families and Community Members,

We, Black Mother Scholars, ask you to pause and think together with us on how we can better protect our children, grandchildren, nieces, nephews, and cousins. As educators, we realize that we have an obligation to share what we know about schools with Black families and communities. We cannot stand by in good conscience as Black children are being hurt every day in deep and long-lasting ways by schools. We share what we know and offer recommendations that we can do in our homes and communities to interrupt Black children's damage. Often, to *protect* our children from pain, we have made the mistake of not telling them about their history from a Black perspective. Our silence does not provide them with the strong foundation that they need to survive the racial violence they will face in school and society. We want you to know that there are positive ways to teach history in a manner that shows the legacy of Black power, perseverance, and ingenuity.

First, we know that you love your children. It's not that we (Black families) do *not* try to protect them. For instance, we

- rejoice when they are born.

- give them strong names.

- move them to "better" neighborhoods when we can.

- take them to places of worship and pray for them every day.

- buy them clothes, digital technologies, and other things that they ask for.

- give them opportunities that we did not have.

- encourage them to learn as much as they can in school.

All of this and more is done in the name of love. In essence, *we be lovin' our children* deeply. Yet, not only are our children and youth (our babies) being shot down by police and would-be vigilantes, but they are subjected to violence every day in school. This may sound unreal, but let us explain and then talk about how we can begin to buffer our children by teaching them (and ourselves) Black history.

Because schools are sites of physical, symbolic, linguistic, curricular/instructional, and systemic suffering[1] for most Black children, our children are actually learning many things that are not good for their spirits, souls, minds, and bodies. As educators and parents, we want to alert families to these hidden types of violence taking place in schools right before our eyes and share ways you can heal your children using Black history. Any of these types of violence *can and do happen to our own children despite our*

- social class,

- social standing,

---

1   These five types of anti-Black violence were outlined in an article; see Johnson et al. (2018).

- geographic region,
- religion,
- skin complexion,
- "proper" home training,
- use of Standard English,
- dress style,
- marital status,
- involvement in school,
- academic achievement level,
- academic track, or
- implementing any other factors that we think will keep our children safe.

Violence in Schools

When someone tells you who they are, believe them the first time.
—Maya Angelou (n.d.)

To be clear, the types of violence that we mention (physical, symbolic, linguistic, curricular/instructional, and systemic) are often disguised and difficult to see. Indeed, they could be classified as being passive-aggressive. But just as White children are not overtly told that they are superior to others (even though the textbooks include disproportionate stories about their history, heroes and heroines, and so forth), Black children are not always directly given the message that they are thought of as inferior. Yet the messages are clear and are ingested by our children without them knowing it.

In the following, we share a few examples of the five types of violence in schools (physical, symbolic, linguistic, curricular/instructional, and systemic), which may escape your notice. Even if your child does not experience all five types of violence, they witness them, which has its own psychological damage. Links to a few, of many, recent examples are provided.

- *Symbolic violence.* Consider Black mother April Carr's story from 2017 (Fortin, 2017). This example demonstrates how Black students' psyches, spirits, and humanity are attacked by negative stereotypes. Black children are also subjected to symbolic violence daily when their voices and experiences are ignored and silenced. **Ever hear a Black child say that he or she does not like his or her skin color?**

- *Systemic violence.* African American children are disproportionately referred to special education classes and are suspended and expelled in significantly greater numbers than their non-Black peers—even in preschool (Editorial Board, 2016)! Systemic violence is embedded in the school structures, policies, and customs, such as tracking, under resourced and overcrowded schools, and zero-tolerance school policies. **Ever heard Black children say that Black children are bad and do not know how to behave in school?**

- *Physical violence.* Sometimes, the violence that our children experience is in the form of a straight-out physical attack. In October 2015, a 16-year-old Black girl in South Carolina was violently thrown from her desk by the school's resource officer as the entire class looked on (Fausset & Southall, 2015). **Ever hear a Black child say they are afraid of the police?**

- *Curricular and instructional violence.* This type of violence is evident in the Whiteness of curriculum, materials, texts, and the absence of normalized teaching of African and African American histories day to day, week to week. Examples include a mock auction in a classroom in New York (Griffith, 2019) and in Georgia during a Civil War reenactment. In sum, Black history is mistaught, distorted, sanitized, and/or omitted in schools. Hence, our children learn that White people are the creators of everything and should be respected. Our children do not learn the rich histories of Black people, our contributions to the United States and to the world historically and contemporarily, or our sense of agency and resistance. **Ever hear a Black child say that Black people are not smart?**

Can Black History Heal Our Children?

Bettina Love, teacher educator at the University of Georgia, says from the moment our Black children enter the school doors, their *spirits* are murdered on a daily basis. We (Gloria and Kamania, along with George Johnson and Udo Uyoata) have suggested that learning African and African American history is an antidote to the ongoing violence that Black children experience in schools. Indeed, we can do more than *talk* about what is hurting our children; we can actually provide tools to heal them. We present a few *starter* ideas for healing our children. Many others are available via an internet search. Our hope is that families will become excited and locate a world of resources to teach Black history. We encourage families and community members to be creative and teach Black history in engaging and interactive ways. The lessons and activities do not have to be long or formal. For instance, you can teach while driving children to school and to extracurricular activities. Importantly, Black history needs to be ongoing, taught, and retaught. Consider spreading the love by working together with other families and community members:

1. **Character development using Adinkra symbols.** To counter symbolic and curricular violence, use Adinkra symbols from West Africa to teach African principles and values that have guided Black people since ancient Africa to contemporary times for Black people worldwide (see http://www.adinkra.org/htmls/adinkra_index.htm). Have children identify Adinkra symbols and values that are important to them (e.g., courage, perseverance, loyalty, wisdom). Find character traits of African and African American people historically and presently. One source is the Smithsonian National Museum of African American History and Culture on social media (https://nmaahc.si.edu/explore/stories).

2. **Readings.** To counter curricular violence, intentionally and routinely provide books and other media that liberate the Black spirit by providing stories written by Black authors and including Black people's perspectives through every historical period.

3. **Africa.** We emphasize that Black history starts in Africa—not with enslavement. Our children need to know that Africa is the cradle of civilization and need to unlearn many negative myths about Africa. We suggest using works of fiction and nonfiction. During every historical and contemporary period, focus on African principles of wisdom, perseverance, self-determination, and Black people's other strengths (see Appendix A to this volume). Over time, try to teach information from the following six overlapping historical periods

(Boutte, 2016). Your children will get the idea of how Black people's strengths have endured across time and space:

- Ancient Africa (e.g., Ethiopia, Kush, Kemet, Ghana, Mali, Songhay)—remember the earliest humans are from Africa.

- Enslavement (1500s–1865)—textbooks will say 1619 (Readers should research this).

- Reconstruction (1865–1877)

- Jim Crow/Segregation (1890–1965/1970)

- Civil Rights/Black Nationalism (1954–1968)

- Contemporary African American and African life and realities (1969–present)

Consider beginning with a geography lesson of the seven continents and then learn more in-depth information about Africa. For example, the song "In My Africa" teaches about the 54 (now 55) countries in Africa and how they are diverse (see Nickwalco, 2013).

You can focus on ancient Kemet (Egypt) and the Ma'at principles: truth, justice, balance, order, compassion, harmony, and reciprocity through discussion, read-alouds, and research. Likewise, it is always fascinating to know that Africa is the cradle of *all* civilization and to study ancient kingdoms so we understand many of the legacies present among African American people today. Children will enjoy role-playing and dressing up as kings, queens, and other citizens in ancient Africa. They will be delighted to learn that the richest man to ever live (to date) was Mansa Musa from Mali.

Final Thoughts

Many Black people are repelled by scenes of African American people being whipped, lynched, or otherwise abused during slavery. Yet we barely blink in the midst of endemic and ongoing spirit murders (Love, 2013) of our children in schools that are taking place in plain view. Indeed, few of us recognize it. Even the best of us fall short amid ongoing violence against our children—especially in schools where they are suspended, expelled, placed in special education, demeaned, and made invisible in the curriculum.

In the Black community, we *love* our children. As we eagerly await them, we give them strong, meaningful, loving names like Stephanie, Jonathan, Janiyah, Jaliyah, Carter, Layla, Dylan, and Langston. We try to protect them—sending them to church, encouraging them to do well in school, carefully selecting their friends, sometimes moving to new neighborhoods if we can afford it. Yet most of us often forget to give them what they need the most to thrive, heal, and survive in a world driven by White supremacy. We fail to teach them their history. In this book, we explain how this can be a fatal oversight in terms of the premature deaths of our children to violence and lifelong, generational damage. This book is based on foundational African legacies that have sustained Black people worldwide since the beginning of time to now (see Appendix A). Learn also about principles for Black education (see Appendix B).

Please do not put this book down if you care about Black children. This is a *pro*-Black book. This is an urgent call to Black families and communities. Recognizing that we are all interconnected, we are not just asking what are we willing to do for our own biological, adopted, or related children but also for all Black children.

In solidarity,

Kamania Wynter-Hoyte and Gloria Swindler Boutte

10

References

Angelou, M. (n.d.). *Maya Angelou quotes*. BrainyQuote. https://www.brainy quote.com/quotes/maya_angelou_383371

Boutte, G. S., Johnson, G. L., Wynter-Hoyt, K., & Uyoata, U. E. (2017). Using African diaspora literacy to heal and restore the souls of Black folks. *International Critical Childhood Policy Studies Journal, 6*(1), 66–79.

Editorial Board. (2016, October 8). *Racial profiling in preschool*. New York Times. https://www.nytimes.com/2016/10/09/opinion/racial-profiling-in-preschool.html

Fausset, R., & Southall, A. (2015, October, 26). *Video shows officer flipping student in South Carolina, prompting inquiry*. New York Times. https://www.nytimes.com/2015/10/27/us/officers-classroom-fight-with-student-is-caught-on-video.html

Fortin, J. (2017, November 8). *Video shows Georgia teacher threatening student: That's how "you get shot."* New York Times. https://www.nytimes.com/2017/11/08/us/georgia-teacher-bullet-shot-video.html

Griffith, J. (2019, May 29). *Black students were cast as slaves in New York teacher's mock "auctions," state finds*. NBC News. https://www.nbcnews.com/news/nbcblk/black-students-were-cast-slaves-new-york-teacher-s-mock-n1011361

Johnson, L., Bryan, N., & Boutte, G. S. (2018). Show us the love: Revolutionary and loving teaching in (un)critical times. *Urban Review*. Advanced online publication. https://doi.org/10.1007/s11256-018-0488-3

Love, B. L. (2016). Anti-Black state violence, classroom edition: The spirit murdering of Black children. *Journal of Curriculum and Pedagogy, 13*(1), 22–25. https://doi.org/10.1080/15505170.2016.1138258

Nickwalco. (2013, October 3). *In my Africa (song on Arthur about the 54 countries in Africa* [Video]. YouTube. https://www.youtube.com/watch?v=pYh-zW3UkS8

2

Jarvais Jackson, Saudah Collins, Janice Baines, and Valente' Gibson

Say It Loud—I'm Black and I'm Proud: Beauty, Brilliance, and Belonging in Our Homes, Classrooms, and Communities

Uh! Your bad self!
Say it loud! I'm black and I'm proud
Say it louder! I'm black and I'm proud
Look a-here!
Some people say we got a lot of malice, some say it's a lotta nerve
But I say we won't quit movin' until we get what we deserve
We've been 'buked and we've been scorned
We've been treated bad, talked about as sure as you're born
But just as sure as it take two eyes to make a pair, huh!
Brother we can't quit until we get our share

—Brown (1969)

James Brown's iconic song "I'm Black and I'm Proud" provides a proclamation that we as Black people should instill in ourselves and our children as we navigate through any space. Honoring and embracing our Blackness is something that we have not often been taught to do. Dating back to 1933, Carter G. Woodson, known as the Father of Black History, asserted Black people are often taught to hate everything

Black and love everything White (Woodson, 1933/1990). When it comes to places such as schools, we have been taught to hide our Blackness through code-switching and other respectability politics. Black people have been taught not to "talk Black" and to suppress other Black cultural expressions. None of this is healthy for us as Black people.

This chapter shares ways that love of Blackness can be celebrated at home and in our communities. Our hope is that Blackness becomes such a strong force in our children that they freely express themselves at school. We share practices that we use in our classrooms as elementary school teachers. Throughout the year, we find ways to teach the seven principles of Kwanzaa (*Nguzo Saba* in Swahili):

- *Umoja*—unity

- *Kujichagulia*—self-determination

- *Ujima*— collective work and responsibility

- *Ujamaa*—cooperative economics

- *Nia*—purpose

- *Kuumba*—creativity

- *Imani*—faith

These seven principles provide a foundational value system that Black children, families, and communities can live by. The learning examples that we share can also be done in Black homes and communities. Some activities cover more than one principle.

Umoja (Unity) and Nia (Purpose)

Fostering unity (togetherness) takes time and a common purpose. Consider focusing on issues that are greater than any one individual. This takes us back to the African principles of communalism rather than individualism. In our classrooms, we use Adinkra symbols from the Akan people in Ghana and Cote D'Ivoire. As students grow to know each other and build a sense of community, we use the Adinkra symbol *nkonsonkonson* (Figure 2.1) as a visual reminder as students think about its chain link.

Figure 2.1. The Adinkra symbol nkonsonkonson
Source: http://www.adinkra.org/htmls/adinkra/nkon.htm

We focus on strengthening bonds by encouraging solidarity, attitudes toward justice, and community in classrooms, schools, homes, and communities. We examine our historical and contemporary connections as Black people through song, dance, visual art, storytelling, and literature studies. Through these activities, our students become more unified and prouder.

Music. Music can play a vital role in connecting to students. We suggest using positive music often to counter negative messages about Black people. In our experiences, most students love music, and they usually learn lyrics to music quite quickly. Using this interest, we often use music in our classrooms to start a dialogue around topics or to share a specific message. Examples of the types of songs used and their particular themes can be found in Table 2.1.

An example using music to engage children and youth in conversations about faith (imani) and self-determination (kujichagulia) can be seen in Baltimore's Cardinal Shehan

15

Table 2.1. Music to Teach Unity and Faith

Title	Artist	Theme
"Tomorrow"	Tevin Campbell (Johnson & Johnson, 1976)	Hope
"Strength, Courage, Wisdom"	India Arie (Simpson, 2000)	Empowerment
"Love's in Need of Love Today"	Stevie Wonder (1976)	Love vs. Hate
"Wake Up Everybody"	John Legend (2010)	Take action
"Black Butterfly"	Deniece Williams (Mann & Well, 1984)	Perseverance
"My Power"	Beyoncé (Ggulu et al., 2019)	Strength
"A Change is Gonna Come"	Sam Cooke (1964)	Triumph
"Glory"	John Legend (Stephens et al., 2014)	Civil Rights

School's performance of Andra Day's "Rise Up" (see WJZ, 2017). We have used the video during morning gatherings to convey the message about standing up in the pursuit of justice. For some students, the song verbalizes feelings they are experiencing as they are exposed to racism through personal experiences and stories they see on the news. For many students, this is a message of hope. After watching the video, we engage students in discussions about how they can work together as a unified force (umoja—unity) to stand up against injustices in their communities and in society.

Music can also be a way to affirm the beauty of Black people. For example, Beyoncé's (2019) "Brown Skin Girl" opens up with

Brown skin girl
Your skin just like pearls
The best thing in the world
never trade you for anybody else

This song serves as a message that Black girls are beautiful and priceless. They often do not hear this in school or in society. Other songs, such as Nas's (2002) "I Can," ignites students' dreams and ambitions reminding them that they can be whatever they put their minds to be (kujichagulia—self-determination). Use these songs, and others, to constantly remind our Black children they are beautiful, powerful, and valuable. Songs like these can be played in the car on the way to school or at home while everyone is getting dressed. Songs can be anthems proclaiming our purpose (nia).

Kujichagulia (Self-Determination)

In our classes, we explore the principle of self-determination in multiple ways gleaning knowledge from many past and present role models throughout the African diaspora such as the widely known story of Rosa Parks to the not-so-well-known story of Sarah Mae Flemming from South Carolina who also refused to sit in the back of a bus. We teach children that it is important to reclaim the ability to define and speak for ourselves. Students learn that affirming messages from their teachers, peers, songs, historical accounts, and literature can help them redefine what it means to be Black and proud. We engage students in dialogue and study about Black hair texture, style, skin tone, language, interactional styles, and clothing selections throughout the year. Ongoing efforts like this are necessary to help Black children and youth transform an internalized Black people's self-determination (kujichagulia). In the following, we provide additional suggestions for exploring the principle of kujichagulia (self-determination).

Contemporary Role Models. Contemporary role models often give relatable examples of how students can develop self-determination. In one of our classes, students learned about the experiences of Kheris Rogers, a young girl tormented by her classmates because of her dark brown skin.

With her family's support, she countered the negative, hateful experience with bold positive messaging of self-love. Kheris started a clothing company with the slogan "Flexin' in My Complexion," which means being proud of one's complexion (*CBS This Morning*, 2018). When Black children learn to value all shades of Blackness, it counters European standards of beauty.

Connecting their interest in sports, we have conversations about athletes and self-determination that allowed them to reach their success. For example, A'ja Wilson, a University of South Carolina women's basketball player, worked through her dyslexia to be a nationally acclaimed professional. At home, engage children in conversations about contemporary role models. Importantly, remember that role models may be family and community members.

Positive Literature. The use of affirming literature can give birth to explorations of Black people naming ourselves and our values and contributions. Through the use of positive literature, children can be inspired by seeing themselves in culturally affirming ways. Remember, *schools often do not include ongoing positive literature about Black people.*

Table 2.2 provides a list of books with affirming messages that would be appropriate for use by children ages 3 through 12. Video read-alouds are also an option and can be found online by doing a Google search. Many more examples can be found on websites like this one: https://aalbc.com/books/children.php.

Visual Art. As we continue to build positive self-identity with literature, affirmations, and music, student engagement and input are vital. At the start of the year, we ask students to introduce themselves and tell their classmates about themselves. Using mirrors to assist with this exploration, students are asked to look at their facial features and then illustrate what they see. These illustrations then become self-portraits.

Table 2.2. Positive Books For Children Ages 3-12

Title	Author	Theme
Ages 3-8		
I Am Enough (Byers, 2018)	Grace Byers	Empowerment
I Am Every Good Thing (Barnes, 2020)	Derrick Barnes	Empowerment
What if…? (Berger, 2018)	Samantha Berger	Inspiration
Hair Love (Cherry, 2019)	Matthew A. Cherry	Uplifting
The Day You Begin (Woodson, 2019)	Jacqueline Woodson	Encouragement
Ages 9-12		
Crown: An Ode to the Fresh Cut (Barnes, 2017)	Derrick Barnes	Empowerment
One Crazy Summer (Williams-Garcia, 2010)	Rita Williams-Garcia	Uplifting
The Parker Inheritance (Johnson 2018)	Varian Johnson	Inspiration
Preaching To The Chickens: The Story of Young (Asim, 2016)	Jabari Asim	Encouragement
The Undefeated (Alexander, 2019)	Kwame Alexander	Resistance

To emphasize the classroom community, the self-portraits are later displayed as art around the classroom. Every day, the students walk in and see themselves. See examples in Figure 2.2.

Figure 2.2. Examples of Students' Self-Portraits

Ujima (Collective Work and Responsibility)

Cultivating a unified learning community that reflects the importance of togetherness and responsibility is important to the foundation of student learning and success. As teachers, we acknowledge that without collective work and struggle, progress and liberation are impossible. We share lessons learned that families and community members can use to explore the principle of Ujima.

Maintain a Focus on "We," Not "I." We use the Adinkra symbol *boa me na me mmoa wo* (Figure 2.3) to focus on commitment, interdependence, cooperation, and the common good. At home and in the community, the focus should not be on the individual. Rather, emphasis should be on the collective with members working together to solve problems and share in the benefits of family or group efforts. These efforts should be rooted in honoring African traditions and practices, such as those shared in Chapter 10. Working collectively brings together knowledge, expertise, strength, and purpose and can foster a greater sense of ownership and pride in one's community.

Figure 2.3. The Adinkra symbol boa me na me mmoa wo. Family time. *Source:* http://www.adinkra.org/htmls/adinkra/boame.htm

If you want to go alone, go fast. If you want to go far, go together.

This African proverb expresses the importance of working together as a collective instead of focusing only on self-achievement. In our classrooms, we create a family atmosphere that allows students to succeed, struggle, and grow collectively. A family is not always blood-related. A family can be people who accept us for who we are and who are willing to support us in our life journeys. Family time is used to celebrate victories or to work through obstacles that have come up. The following suggestions emphasize the importance of togetherness and responsibility for families and communities:

- Take time to talk—Dedicate time to talk without distractions (e.g., electronics, television).

- Record family stories—Build family histories by recording the stories and memoirs of family members and community members (i.e., time spent at a local store or restaurant, barbershop, or beauty salon or time spent doing family traditions such as holidays or Sunday dinners).

- Community and family timelines—Children can interview family members and make an illustrated timeline of the most important family events and memories.

- Name storybook—Children can interview family members and create a family name storybook (e.g., Where did I get my name from? Who helped name me?).

Conclusion

While there is no one way to reach the ultimate goal of embracing Black beauty and brilliance, we hope that these examples provide starting points and ideas to use. Of course, these examples should be tailored to the needs of families, classrooms, and community settings. Importantly, we advise not avoiding conversations on what it means to be Black and proud and to love Blackness.

References

Alexander, K. (2019). *The undefeated*. Houghton Mifflin Harcourt.

Asim, J. (2016). *Preaching to the chickens: The story of Young*. Nancy Paulsen Books.

Barnes, D. (2020). *I am every good thing*. Nancy Paulsen Books.

Barnes, D. (2017). *Crown: The ode to the fresh cut*. Agate Bolden.

Berger, S. (2018). *What if . . .* Little, Brown Books for Young Readers.

Beyoncé. (2019). Brown skin girl [Song]. On *The lion king: The gift*. Parkwood Entertainment LLC.

Brown, J. (1969). Say it loud - I'm Black and I'm proud [Song]. On *Say it loud - I'm Black and I'm proud*. UMG.

Byers, G. (2018). *I am enough*. Balzer & Bray.

CBS This Morning. (2018, July 31). *Flexin' in my complexion: 11-year-old transforms bullying experience into success* [Video]. YouTube. https://www.youtube.com/watch?v=pKa44qL_8Zs

Cherry, M. A. (2019). *Hair love*. Kokila.

Cooke, S. (1964). A Change is Gonna Come. On *Ain't That Good News*. RCA Victor: Hollywood, CA.

Gqulu, B. B., Twisha, S., Charles, A. C., & Gwala, L. (2019). Strength. On *Lion King: The Gift*. Parkwood/ Columbia: New York, NY.

Johnson, G., & Johnson, L. (1976). Tomorrow (A Better You, Better Me). On *Look Out for #1*. Santa Monica, CA: A & M Records.

Johnson, V. (2018). *The Parker inheritance*. Arthur A. Levine Books.

Legend, J. (2010). Wake Up!. On *The Roots*. GOOD/Columbia: New York, NY.

Mann, B., & Well, C. (1984). Black Butterfly. On *Let's Hear it for the Boys*. Columbia: New York, NY.

Nas. (2002). I can [Song]. On *God's son*. Sony.

Simpson, I. A. (2000). Strength, Courage, & Wisdom. On *Bamboozled*. New York, New York: Warner Chappell Music.

Stephens, J., Lynn, L., & Smith, C. (2014). Glory. On *Selma soundtrack*. ARTium/ Def Jam/Columbia: New York, NY.

Williams-Garcia, R. (2010). *One crazy summer*. HarperCollins.

WJZ. (2017, October 12). *Students from Baltimore's Cardinal Shehan School sing "Rise Up"* [Video]. YouTube. https://www.youtube.com/watch?v= IEGEovFX534

Wonder, S. (1976). Love's in Need of Love Today. On *Songs in the Key of Life*. Los Angeles: Tamla/Motown.

Woodson, C. G. (1990). *The mis-education of the Negro*. Africa World Press. (Original work published 1933)

Woodson, J. (2019). *The day you begin*. Penguin Young Readers Group.

3

*Shaquetta Moultrie, Antoinette Gibson,
and Julia Dawson*

Great Rising: Activities to Inspire Black Teens and Youth[1]

Black Girl Magic Project—Shaquetta Moultrie

Michelle Obama. Beyoncé. Simone Biles. Rihanna. This is a concise list of successful Black women. I could write a book outlining their accomplishments. Michelle Obama, first lady and woman of the millennium (as far as we are concerned)—children, teens, and adults admire her. Beyoncé has a following so huge that when she performed at the Super Bowl, people on social media said there was a football game at the "Beyoncé concert." Simone Biles's talent and determination have made her a top gymnast globally, winning four Olympic gold medals. Rihanna, a young talent from Barbados, is the world's wealthiest female singer, owning both makeup and lingerie lines, Fenty and Savage, respectively. She also started the Clara Lionel Foundation to fund education projects and health and emergency response following disasters worldwide.

But you don't have to be famous to possess "Black Girl Magic." All Black women have it. I'm not saying that magic

---

1   Activities in this chapter are focused on Black youth ages 11 to 16, but youth of different ages may also enjoy them.

is not in everyone, but that's just not my current focus. The wonders and beauty of Black and Brown women have been suppressed, covered up, even buried. Children are vulnerable and impressionable. Popular social media, television, magazine images, and so on shape how beauty is defined in society. In modern U.S. history, that definition did not include dark skin, kinky-curly hair, full lips, and full, curvy figures. Instead, these images show light, bright, damn-near white skin, long silky hair, and slim, straight-figured women with thin lips covered in red lipstick.

Chimamanda Adichie, a Nigerian American author, speaks about the dangers of a single story about any group of people and how this creates stereotypes. How a story is told, who tells it, the audience, and how often it's said can make that story dangerous. In the case of stories about the beauty or lack thereof, in Black women—they've been told so much, for so long, by so many people, to so many people—that it's embedded in our Black and Brown girls' psyches. They don't believe they are supermodel pretty.

C'mon, how many of our daughters aspire to be dark-skinned sisters like Maria Borges, Nyakim Gatwech, or Alek Wek? We must teach our daughters, sisters, nieces, and cousins about Black Girl Magic because society won't. Society shares a single story. Until we become the authors, coming from different perspectives, Black girls will believe the tale that deflects their beauty and diminishes their pride.

Let me tell you a story. It starts with a small girl who was her mother's firstborn and the second born to her father. She and her sister were like ebony and ivory. She was a smooth chocolate brown; her sister was often asked if she was "mixed with White." The ebony daughter, at the young age of 5, despised her complexion. When she purchased dolls, she wanted the "tan"-colored toy. One day, her mother asked, "Why don't you like darker dolls?" Her daughter called them "ugly." Immediately, the mother knew they needed to have a longer talk. In the conversation that followed, she learned that her daughter wanted lighter skin and freckles. She wanted to look more like her sister because everyone called her sister "pretty." This was heartbreaking for her mother to hear. Her mother knew something had to be done, but she was confused, filled with questions: "When did this configuration in the Brown girl's brain happen?" How and why did it happen?"

The young girl in this story is my daughter. Had I not sat down with her after that store visit, I would never have known that she didn't feel worthy in her own skin. We live in a technological age where social media largely idolizes the *opposite* of Brown girls, and they feel this. This is why we must become a narrator in our girls' lives. We have to speak to the profound beauty in them—expose them to something other than the single story they're told. With that in mind, I propose the following activities, which I have titled **The Black Girl Magic Project**. (Boys may also do them.)

Activity 1: The Danger of a Single Story
Have children watch the 19-minute TED Talk on YouTube *The Danger of a Single Story* with Chimamanda Ngozi Adichie (https://www.ted.com/talks/chimamanda_ngozi_adichie_the_danger_of_a_single_story?language=en). Adichie speaks on how society sees and hears one side of a story, and this story shapes and defines what is. Adichie is from Nigeria, West Africa. Before starting the video, ask children what they know about Africa (i.e., What is it like? How do the people look? How do they live?). After the video, ask them if they still believe everything they thought before. Why or why not? Have them think about and discuss how society has labeled Black people. Using this information, let the child(ren) create a word collage on stereotypes about Black people. Discuss where they got this story and how it could be dangerous to

youth who believe it. Then have children create a collage depicting a new story—one with positive words describing Black people. Finally, engage in dialogue about why it's important for Black people to grow and learn more about themselves and where our ancestors come from.

Activity 2: Introduction to Black Girl Magic

Ask the child(ren) what they know about the Black Girl Magic movement. After this discussion, have them look up the Black Girl Magic movement to learn more information, such as the founder, what it means, and why it began. Finally, have them write a poem about what Black Girl Magic means to them (see http://www.blackgirlmagicmag.com/about-1).

Activity 3: Shades of Magic

In this activity, have the child(ren) look through Black publications to find various Black women (or teens or children) with success stories. Suggested magazines include *Essence, Ebony, Black Beauty, PRIDE*, and *Today's Black Woman*. Once they find the pictures, they will create a poster with the women's names and achievements. This activity exposes children to the diverse looks and shades of Black women to instill in them that Black is beautiful. It will also allow them to see diversity in the types of successes Black women have. You don't have to be a movie star or singer to be successful. You can be an author, teacher, parent, politician, veterinarian, entrepreneur, and a thousand other possibilities. Black Girl Magic flows in many different ways.

Activity 4: Where They Get That From?

In this activity, children research how many things in popular culture are rooted in Africa. They can consider hair, music, and dance for starters. For example, children will find that braids existed in ancient Africa, are common in contemporary Africa, and are now extremely popular in the United States. This activity aims to shift the mindset of the single story and show that there are many African cultures, not just one, and they've influenced African Americans since our ancestors first came to the United States.

Activity 5: You Got That Black Girl Magic

In this activity, the children will think about women in their lives and list Black girl magic attributes they possess. This activity aims to teach our youth about lifting each other up rather than tearing each other down, understanding that beauty comes in many different shapes, forms, and fashions. It also emphasizes learning about past generations.

Activity 6: I Got That Black Girl Magic—The Beauty in YOU

In this final activity, children will create an autobiography. They will discuss their own personal success stories. Whether they're good at writing, drawing, painting, singing...whatever! The goal is to highlight their own beauty. This can be completed by creating a PowerPoint presentation or writing a book or short story. Invite them to include pictures of themselves with captions. Encourage them to share their stories.

Tearing down the boundaries that define beauty and building up Black girls' confidence is a necessity. Cashawn Thompson said she started the Black Girl Magic movement to honor girls and women relatives and friends that were doing things so incredible that it seemed magical to her (Black Girl Magic, 2020). Her movement blew up on social media. This activity aims to help young girls everywhere recognize themselves and the magical things they do that go unnoticed every day.

Black Malehood and Freedom—Antoinette Gibson

After my third year as a teacher, I had an alarming discovery. I noticed that African American males were not being stimulated academically. I also saw how many Black male students were receiving special education services. I realized that African American males are more engaged during kinesthetic, or tactile, learning activities. Therefore, I recommend inviting Black male teens to move, draw, dance, sing, or express themselves in other ways—physically and orally.

One way adults can be forces of healing in Black boys' lives is by making nonjudgmental spaces for them to fully express themselves. Five such activities are offered next.

Activity 1: Bruh Genius

Sample prompts such as the following ones can help Black boys learn and express themselves:

- What are your learning preferences?

- What do you like and not like about school based on your experiences so far?

- Describe what you already know about the history and art forms created by African Americans from the 1600s to now.

Engage the young men in discussion about their answers. Share African traditions of storytelling and oral art forms and discuss the importance of Black people expressing ourselves. Here's one resource: *The Legacy of Storytelling in African-American History* from *CBS This Morning* (https://www.youtube.com/watch?v=I5hth0VvSyA).

Activity 2: Lyrical Swagger

Play clean versions of Lil Baby's "The Bigger Picture" (https://www.youtube.com/watch?v=v7GrlW3y_r0) and Trey Songz's "2020 Riots: How Many Times?" (https://www.youtube.com/watch?v=wWz1LI1aF-A). Talk with the teens about injustice and how these Black male artists use intellectual and creative oral communication skills to speak persuasively about it.

Activity 3: Research Time

Tell youth you're now going to jump from 2020, back through U.S. history to 1961 through 1974. Help them create a timeline that displays at least four to six historical events of the Black Freedom Movement between 1961 and 1974. Here are some resources:

- Zinn Education Project (Black nationalist, People's Movement): https://www.zinnedproject.org/materials /?s=black+nationalist&cond[0]=period_str:1961

- Stanford University. The Martin Luther King, Jr. Research and Education Institute: https://kinginstitute. stanford.edu/encyclopedia/black-nationalism

Next, let youth do a Google search and find short, informative, accurate, and engaging videos from or about the 1961–1974 period for the state you live in. The videos should go along with the timeline events.

Activity 4: Image Search

Ask youth to do a Google search for three to five pictures of the civil rights/Black nationalist movements between 1961 and 1974. Ask them to write the date and describe what different images show. Talk about the answers with your child, or have them draw and fill out the chart in Table 3.1 for each picture.

Table 3.1. Image Search

Picture and date picture was taken	What story does the picture tell? What does it mean? Why does it matter?
	Tell: Mean: Matter:

Activity 5: Say It Loud, Black, and Proud

Youth will use background knowledge from their research, timeline, videos, and pictures to create a story about the history they researched. They'll compare the history to their own lives today as young Black male teens in the United States. They can use Lil Baby's and Trey Songz's songs as models. The teens then turn their stories into a poem, rap, song, essay, speech, poster, or another format that they choose. Invite the teens to share their work with you at family or other events.

Cherishing Black Children's Names—Julia Dawson

The Color Purple author Alice Walker, boxer Muhammad Ali, and the Muslim minister and activist Malcolm X—all of them examined their names. Alice Walker chose to keep her birth name. Ali and Malcolm X changed theirs. These are three examples of *millions* of messengers of Black love and power.

The power to name holds within it many other powers. The What's in MY Name project invites Black teens to research the stories of their names to reclaim or cherish the African and African American legacies alive in them. Before starting, read through the activities yourself to better guide your teen.

Activity 1: My Blackness. My Name: Where I Am Right Now

Ask these questions. Take notes or record children's answers as a family keepsake.

1. Do you call yourself Black? Why or why not?

2. What does the word *Black*, as in Black people, mean to you?

3. What do you know about your full name? How do you feel about it?

Invite the child to share out loud and/or create a drawing, poem, or song using supplies like paint and paper or a cellphone app such as TikTok.

Activity 2: Malcolm X and "Slave Names"

Listen to a short clip from one famous, often misrepresented, Black American: the Muslim minister, activist, and pan-Africanist Malcolm X. The clip shows a little about him, but there's *much* more to learn!

Ask your child what they already know about him. Use *BLACKPAST, Malcolm X (1925–1965)* (https://www.blackpast. org/african-american-history/x-malcolm-1925-1965/) to learn more. If your teen labels him "hateful," discuss how and why people like Malcolm X have been misrepresented. This is a chance to focus on how he showed Black love and power. Have children watch *Malcolm X: Slave Names* (https://www. youtube.com/watch?v=MBtZwVioc_I&t=3s&pbjreload=101). After listening, ask children to answer the questions on paper and/or discuss it together:

1. List two main ideas Malcolm X makes in this clip.

2. What is Malcolm X saying about African Americans' last names?

3. Would you ever want to change your name? Why or why not?

Activity 3: Naming Traditions From Different African Groups

Read with your teen *This Is How Traditional Naming Ceremonies Are Performed Across the African Diaspora* (Malik, 2018). Read this resource over 2 days. Consider focusing on the parts in Table 3.2. Discuss, audio record, or invite your teen to write answers.

Table 3.2. Questions About African Names and Naming Ceremonies

Describe three details of the Edo naming ceremony. What are examples of Edo names?	
What do the Yoruba people believe about the meaning of a child's name? What are at least two reasons the naming ceremony is so important?	
When must the Akan naming ceremony occur? How is water used in the ceremony? What are examples of Akan names?	

Activity 4: "Know Thyself"

Now your child will research her/his name!

1. Write three to six interview questions together.

2. Decide who to interview. Have them call those relatives/friends.

3. Video, audio record, or listen and take notes during the interview(s).

4. Invite the teen to use the interview(s) to create a speech, poem, rap, dance, painting, collage using PowerPoint, a WordPress webpage, or an actual poster all about their name. It can include pictures and words about their name's meaning and history, plus how it connects to African and African American traditions. Figure 3.1 is one example.

After the project, ask, "Have your views about who you are or Black people and history changed? If yes, how?" To share your experiences, use this link: https://docs.google.

Figure 3.1. Sample of Name Research Activity

com/forms/d/e/1FAIpQLSf5FBPMOxEvmd0T2ePC7n9Uquc
4j9H6nJkYLBHoo96-GTOS4A/viewform.

References

Black Girl Magic. (2020). *Black girls are magic. The movement.*https://www.
        godaddy.com/garage/how-one-woman-started-a-movement-with-
        blackgirlmagic/

Malik, A. (2018). *This is how traditional naming ceremonies are performed
        across the African diaspora.* The Pan-African Alliance. https://www.
        panafricanalliance.com/african-renaming-ceremonies/

Preparing Black Children to Identify and Confront Racism in Books, Media, and Other Texts: Critical Questions

This chapter offers questions to empower Black children to identify and confront messages that distort or omit information about African and African American history, people, and communities. These critical questions are suited for children of all ages. They can examine books, advertisements, music, television, movies, and other media content for racially discriminating language, illustrations, and story lines. Critical questions are one way that Black adults can help buffer Black children from anti-Black racism.

What Black Children Are Learning About Themselves

The Adinkra symbol *mate masie* (pronounced Mah-ti Mah-see-eh) means "What I hear, I keep" (Figure 4.1), symbolizes knowledge, wisdom, and the prudence of taking into consideration what another person has shared in our journey to gain information, knowledge, and understanding. At the same time, taken literally, the symbol implies that what people are told (and hear) can have a deep, long-lasting influence on them. This is particularly true of children since they are impressionable. While comments from parents often make strong impressions on children, so do messages in books, movies, television, music, conversations, and other texts. All these influences can impact children's perceptions of themselves.

Figure 4.1. Adinkra symbol mate masie, "What I hear, I keep," a symbol of wisdom, knowledge, and prudence.
Source: http://www.adinkra.org/htmls/adinkra/mate.htm

Black families often shine a light on children's brilliance. However, when children go to school, they are likely to see negative portrayals of Black people and their potential. Additionally, research shows that Black children are regularly over-referred to special education, under-referred to gifted programs, and unfairly disciplined. Black history, language, and culture are often omitted or misrepresented in school curricula. As a matter of fact, Black children often first see themselves represented in school textbooks as people who are enslaved and then not again till the limited appearance of very incomplete descriptions of a few well-known (dead) Black people such as Dr. Martin Luther King Jr., Harriet Tubman, Rosa Parks, and others. The long history of African people that spans thousands of years is often not covered in school. These negative and omitted examples of Black experiences can cause personal, psychological, and spiritual injuries to children.

What Can Do Done to Keep Black Children's Self-Esteem Intact?

First, it is essential to know that Black people have always been actively working on letting children know that they are "Young, Gifted, and Black" and to keep "their souls intact." For example, African American communities have published books describing Black brilliance, purchased and shared positive Black books with their children, produced radio and television programs to counter negative racial messages, organized public protests, and led legal challenges to improve their community schools.

Second, children have historically been part of many of these efforts. In the 1920s, Black children had been featured in publications that countered racist issues (e.g., W. E. B. Du Bois & Fauset's, 1920-1921, *Brownies' Book*; Shackelford's, 1944, *My Happy Days*; and Tarry and Ets's, 1946, *My Dog Rinty*). Black children have been actors on groundbreaking television programs that called out systemic racism. An early example is the 1960s' *Inside Bed-Stuy*, in which Black children chanted, "What has America done for me? Nothing, but made me a zombie—I don't know who I am!" (Cole, 2003, "From Belafonte to Black Power"). Perhaps the most famous example of children protesting is the Children's Crusade in Birmingham, Alabama, during May 1963. During this time, thousands of African American children walked out of school and marched for civil rights.

Today, we once again see Black children confronting injustice as they march in #BlackLivesMatter protests and produce their own antiracist content on social media. This chapter's critical questions will help Black children push back against words and texts that try to negatively depict or misrepresent their life experiences and culture.

Black Children Are Aware of Injustices

Every parent knows that children ask questions at a relentless pace. These questions often show children's innate ability to discern fairness, injustice, and power. For example, children may ask, "Why does my friend have a later bedtime than me?" or "Why does my brother get to pick what game we play?" Children also address more weighty issues such as "Why is COVID-19 affecting more Black people?" and "Why do police kill unarmed Black people?" The children's keen understanding of fairness, justice, and inequity is the basis for critical questions.

Critical Questions That Can Help Discuss Racism With Children and Youth

Black children and youth need to know that they can question what they read, see, and hear. When children ask critical questions, they embody the Adinkra symbol, mate masie, a symbol of wisdom, knowledge, and good judgment. As Black children learn the art of taking critical stances, they understand that they do not have to agree with what is written in books or shown in the media and the world about Black people. Children and youth become detectives in noticing whose voices are prioritized, minimized, or overlooked. Following are sample questions and prompts that can help children recognize racism and other types of injustices in books, television, music, video games, movies, social media, different types of texts, and life:

- Are Black people included in this text? Why or why not?

- Do you see anything unfair to Black people? Tell me more about this.

- Who or what is shown as necessary? How was the message of importance conveyed?

- Are Black people left out or shown as unimportant? How was this message conveyed?

- Can this message be hurtful or unfair to Black people? Why?

- How does the text make you feel? Why?

- What can you do to improve this issue?

At first, adults might need to lead children through the questions as they look critically at advertisements, books, and media. Eventually, children can use these questions as a lens through which they process everyday interactions.

What Are Advertisements Selling?

The American Academy of Pediatrics reports that children see upward of 40,000 advertisements a year (American Psychological Association, 2004). We know that many of these contain images and words that can damage African American children's self-image—even if they are not aware of it. Encouraging children to use critical questions can transform passive or subconscious acceptance of these messages to active rejection and confrontation.

In addition to advertisements selling the products they feature, they also can sell harmful racist messages. The following three examples show how critical questions can be used to confront detrimental and dangerous advertisements.

1. In a Dove body wash advertisement, a Black woman pulls a shirt over her head and emerges as a White woman (Chan, 2017). Asking children if they see anything unfair and who is shown as important can help

children detect if the ad is suggesting that a soap that "gets you whiter" is glorifying White people. Asking children who is left out or shown as unimportant or who might find this image to be hurtful or unfair can help children identify that this advertisement diminishes Black people's dignity and worth.

2. A similar example is an advertisement for Gap Kids in which the elbow of a tall White child rests on the head of the shorter child standing next to her. The shorter girl is the only Black child in the photo. While this ad was supposed to champion female empowerment, it degrades the only Black person in the advertisement by posturing her like "an armrest" for the taller White child (Kim, 2016). Again, the critical questions can help children call out this racist imagery.

3. Finally, Kellogg's Corn Pops cereal printed a game on the back of the box, showing a shopping mall filled with colorful cartoon characters shaped like corn kernels. The characters are sunbathing, shopping, playing, taking photos, and skateboarding. Juxtaposed to these fun images is the only Brown-skinned character who is a janitor cleaning the floors (*Ad Age*, 2017). While explaining to children that there is nothing wrong with being a janitor, the critical questions can help children confront the negative racial message featured in this illustration.

Judge a Book by Its Cover and Words

Children are often warned not to judge a book by its cover, meaning that outward appearances are often not inner-worth indicators. However, when it comes to books (and other forms of information—including cartoons), children *should* judge them by their covers and every page. Time and again, young children's picture books and older children's textbooks contain anti-Black content. It is no wonder that too many Black children end up internalizing negative messages about Black people. Critical questions can help children critique these books.

For example, I share four of an endless number of books, including damaging anti-Black messages. Exhibit 1—*The House That George Built* (Slade, 2015)—describes how George Washington built the White House but barely mentions the significant role that African American people who were enslaved had in the building's physical construction. In Exhibits 2 and 3—*A Birthday Cake for George Washington* (Ganeshram, 2016, which was recalled by Scholastic for its unrealistic depictions) and *A Fine Dessert: Four Centuries, Four Families, One Delicious Treat* (Jenkins, 2015)—African American people who were enslaved are portrayed as smiling and seemingly happy with their situation. Exhibit 4—another example is found in a Texas state-approved high school geography book. Under a heading "Patterns of Immigration," the text describes the European slave trade as having brought "millions of *workers* from Africa to the southern United States to work on agricultural plantations" (Fernandez & Hauser, 2015, p. 10). With more than 100,000 copies of the book published, many African American children undoubtedly have been misled about the brutal history of Europeans' role in Black people's enslavement.

In each of these cases, the critical questions can help children detect what is racist and anti-Black. The more practice children have with critically questioning books, media, and other information, the more we can help them resist negative messages about Black people. They can actively learn to seek books and other texts that tell stories from Black people's perspective.

Reading the World

Currently, schools overfocus on teaching children to be passive producers and consumers of knowledge. In other words, children are told to accept whatever information is given—even when it is not accurate or contains negative stereotypes. Students are often not educated to use critical thinking to read texts to understand anti-Blackness and racism. Yet these critical thinking skills are crucial for Black children to confront racism and promote antiracism. Since this stance is not enacted by many teachers or schools, families need to empower their children to critically question the world around them.

What I Hear, I Keep

As long as racism is present, Black children need opportunities to name, question, confront, and work toward Black people's liberation. Critical questions can be used by children to talk back to anti-Black images and ideas. Families cannot always protect children from what they hear, but they can empower children to understand that not everything written or uttered needs to be kept. This is the essence of mate masie (wisdom).

References

Ad Age. (2017, October 25). *Marketer's brief: Kellogg accused of racist Corn Pops packaging*. https://adage.com/article/cmo-strategy/marketer-s-kellogg-s-accused-racist-packaging/311029

American Psychological Association. (2004, February 20). *Advertising and children*. http://www.apa.org/pubs/info/reports/advertising-children

Chan, M. (2017, October 9). *Dove's "racist" ad isn't the first time the company was criticized for being offensive*. Time. https://time.com/4974452/dove-ad-facebook-racist/

Cole, W. (2003, April–May). *Anomaly tv: Inside Bed-Stuy*. The Brooklyn Rail. https://brooklynrail.org/2003/04/local/anomaly-tv-inside-bed-stuy

Du Bois, W. E. B., & Fauset, J. (Eds.). (1920). *The Brownies' book: A monthly magazine for children of the sun*. 24 vols. Du Bois & Dill.

Fernandez, M., & Hauser, C. (2015, October 5). *Texas mother teaches textbook company a lesson on accuracy*. The New York Times.

Ganeshram, R. (2016). *A birthday cake for George Washington*. Scholastic.

Jenkins, E. (2015). *A fine dessert: Four centuries, four families, one delicious treat*. Random House Children's Books.

Kim, S. (2016, April 6). *Gap pulls ad called "racist," apologizes to critics*. ABC News. https://abcnews.go.com/Business/gap-pulls-ad-called-racist-apologizes-critics/story?id=38190519

Shackelford, J. D. (1944). *My happy days*. The Associated Publishers. Inc.

Slade, S. (2015). *The house that George built*. Charlesbridge.

Tarry, E., & Ets, M. H. (1946). *My dog Rinty*. Viking Press.

Ricardo Neal and Kindel Nash

Each One, Teach One: Reflections and Lessons on Mentoring Young Men of Color

Figure 5.1. *Aya*: resourcefulness and endurance
Source: http://www.adinkra.org/htmls/adinkra/aya.htm

To My Boys, I haven't yet entirely told you my story and why I've dedicated my life to serving you. This chapter is a letter to you. I write it because I want to share the story of how I came to the work of mentoring and supporting young men, and why I think your success is an essential ingredient to building vibrant communities. For you and all those that read this, I hope you see how *each one can teach one*. Aya is the West African Adinkra symbol representing the fern (see Figure 5.1). Ferns are hardy plants that can grow in difficult places. There are lessons to be shared, and I hope you can use them as you grow and consider how you might best serve others. It has been my honor to serve you, and I commend you for your strength in the face of adversity.

Ricardo Owen Neal
Founder and Chief Executive Officer
We Will All Rise, Inc.

Early Years: Jamaica

Boys,[1] the 11-year-old boy who came to the United States so many summers ago is ever-present in who I am, what I do, and how I do what I do. Living in Jamaica was idyllic and sad at the same time. I lived with both my parents and my seven siblings. We had a wonderful house with indoor plumbing, a washroom, and a veranda that wrapped around the house's front. I would say there was a back veranda, but my older siblings would likely tell me that my memory is off. The details have become foggy over the decades.

In Jamaica, we raised pigs, chickens, and goats. We grew sugarcane, almonds, cherries, coconuts, mangos, and other fruits and vegetables that have escaped my memory. I remember the wash lady coming to help my mother and the guy who would cut the grass with a machete. We were happy in Jamaica. Our seven national heroes were Black women and men, and they were fierce. They built a vibrant culture, and we reveled in our beauty and success. Teachers, doctors, bankers, politicians, lunch ladies, taxi drivers, and entertainers were all Black, brilliant, beautiful, and proud.

Yet, for all that Jamaica had to offer, my parents knew they had to leave. Education ends in eighth grade if students fail to pass the high school common entrance exam. Jamaica was a violent place in the 1980s because of deep-rooted conflicts between the People's National Party and the Jamaican Labour Party. I remember the rat-a-tat-tat of machine guns at night, gunmen running through our property, all of us huddled

---

1   The use of the word *boy* should not be mistaken as a sign of disrespect. When I use the word, there is a history of mutual respect and admiration that the young men will understand.

together in my parents' room. When it was not the real risk of gun slaughter, it was an entire community running, chests heaving from the suffocating smell of sulfuric acid blanketing the community. We had to leave our home despite its beauty and affirming images of brilliance and success.

Middle Years: Finding a New Home and Discovering Hate

We arrived in Lawrence, Massachusetts, during the mid-1980s. Historic mills, massive, sturdy, and repurposed, dominated the city. What struck me about Lawrence were the flags lining Essex Street. In my mind, the flags represented respect for diverse cultures. They meant that all were welcomed regardless of national origin. The flags suggested that there was a home for everyone in Lawrence. Yet I realized something else—for the first time in my life—everyone was not Black. I felt alone and outside for the first time ever, but I was okay because I went home to a strong family every day.

I started cleaning up city parks and rivers and got involved in student government. I cared about my new home. I wanted to do my part to improve Lawrence. Still, I quickly learned that not everyone in my community actually wanted me or my help. I can still remember an older White lady telling me to "go back to where you are from" after a school committee meeting. There was also a time when I was walking home, and a bunch of White boys said something about "the nigger." That was my first time hearing the word. I knew it was a terrible thing, yet I didn't overthink about those boys. The foundation for loving and taking care of my community was firmly established. I already knew I had a voice, and I had every intention of using it.

I enrolled in the University of Massachusetts at Amherst, and the nigger thing followed me to campus. How should a young man react to find the word nigger and human feces smeared on his dorm room door? Frankly, I felt protected by the Black community and other students of color who felt rage and wanted to be left alone just to live. I refused to let hate and ignorance consume me. There was too much to be done. By the time I left college, I was secure in my identity as a leader and an advocate. More important, I'd accomplished more than my parents ever imagined possible.

In the Now: The Power of Love and Community

Gentlemen, as I reflect on lessons learned from my two decades of mentoring work, I now realize that I have spent most of my time in communities fighting hate. The closer my community work took me to street outreach—visiting jails, talking to young men about their lives—the more I realized that our Black boys and other people of color seemed to be dying at an alarming rate. In fact, one out of every 1,000 young Black men is the fatal victim of police violence. At the same time, other young men and women of color are also more likely to die at the police's hands (Edwards et al., 2019). As I visited juvenile detention centers and prisons, the stark reality was that Black men were the primary occupants. At the same time, the community was fighting to save their lives. I had no choice but to join the fight. I sat on various boards and partnered with law enforcement. I encouraged folks in my circle to get involved. Over time, I settled on education as the most meaningful way to impact change. My combined experiences led me to found We Will All Rise (All Rise), an organization focused on mentoring young men of color and dedicated to educating, elevating, and empowering our community members to surmount social, economic, and institutional barriers.

Advice to Young Men Rising

Boys, I wanted to share my story because as you chart your course in life, I want you to recognize that, like aya, the fern, we can grow and emerge stronger from difficult circumstances.

We go about our fight for justice in different ways, but we must be unified in our efforts at the end of the day, always showing respect for our brothers. Joyce King (2005) highlighted the principle that "we exist as African People, an ethnic family. Our perspective must be centered in that reality" (p. 20). With this knowledge of the importance of viewing ourselves as a family whose collective survival is more important than individual survival, I offer these words of advice to you as you consider ways to join together in the fight and carry forward the mentoring work:

- You will have justified anger, and some of you will take to the streets to push back hard against hate. I salute you in your fight.

- Some of you will use the written word to fight back against disinformation and misrepresentation. Well-meaning White allies will want to change your words to fit their narrative. Resist that approach at all times because they do not know your struggle, and they often perpetuate negative stereotypes.

- Those who take to the pulpit—your words and actions are divine, not because of you but because you have been chosen as a vessel to deliver God's words. You are our spiritual warriors because we need unconditional love and protection.

- Gentlemen, elevate and champion those waging the fight inside corporate America, where brothers are often fighting the good fight in isolation, misunderstood by professional peers, and considered a "sell-out" by many.

- We are one community on many different paths to right the wrongs that have been wrought upon us. Love and respect for each other. Do not tear each other down in the fight.

Ubuntu: Mentoring Men of Color

Nobel Peace Prize-winner Desmond Tutu (1999) remarked, "When we want to give high praise to someone, we say, 'Yu u nobuntu' [So-and-so has ubuntu]" (p. 31). Ubuntu is a South African principle that means "humanness." Exhibiting ubuntu is carried out by prioritizing relationships with others, so it is associated with the phrase "I am because we are" (Metz, 2011). When thinking about mentoring Black and other young men of color, I have learned the most important lesson is to prioritize relationships with the boys as the center of the work. That is why most of this chapter is a letter to the boys. In this section, building foremost on ubuntu's principle, we lay out foundational ideas that have been important, hoping others can build on it in doing mentoring work:

- **Build an ecosystem.** Consider how you might engage barbershops, convenience stores, religious institutions, schools, gyms, or other businesses.

- **Engage women.** In our experience, Black men will not succeed unless Black women succeed. Black women will lead in critical ways that demand respect and support.

- **Create rituals and celebrations.** It is essential to believe in the brilliance of young Black men. Let them know that they will face setbacks in life, yet significant things await. Publicly celebrate them to showcase their gifts. Create annual events like dinners and tie-tying ceremonies to celebrate mentoring activities. Share written pieces that honor Black men and encourage them to create original works. Without exception, always honor those who walked the path with you when mentoring young Black men.

- **Be accessible to younger brothers.** Those who are younger than you will admire you and want to emulate what you have accomplished. Respond with love and appreciation when a young man wants to be in your presence. Listen carefully when a more youthful brother approaches you. He may not have all the right words, but he wants to learn. Help him understand the value of being healthy and productive, for he wants to become a responsible man.

- **Explore and experiment with the unfamiliar.** Engage mentees through going to plays, athletic events, and participating in service events together. Travel to new places (domestically and internationally) whenever you have a chance. Interacting with different cultures and communities will strengthen minds and souls and increase the commitment to creating a better world.

- **Hold each other accountable.** Get to know the brothers you support. Set expectations based on their life circumstances and call them out when they fail to meet those expectations. When you know that they can process your feedback, help young brothers to self-correct. Point them to resources when you do not have the answers. Do not tear down your brothers.

- **Stay the course.** You will become angry when young brothers do not heed your advice. They will make life-altering mistakes and disappointment will set in. It is in the most challenging moments where you double down (pull back when necessary but do not abandon) and let them know that you love them and stand ready to support them when they are right.

I (Ricardo) encourage those of you who do mentoring work to find your brothers' and sisters' band as you assume greater responsibilities in your life. They will stand with you when you confront difficult times. For almost a decade now, four Black men, Ivan Douglas, Mark Nash, LaVaughn Turner, and Maurice Wilkins, have been my partners in this beautiful struggle and, most recently, Calvin Lewis. I honor each man because they have been tireless in their work with a fierce commitment to young men of color. Finally, while the reality of a brilliant and vibrant Black culture in Jamaica is seared in my memory, I have faced anti-Black hate and oppression in this country. Yet I am like the fern, aya, growing in a difficult place, and I fight because I have been offered many opportunities in America. I refuse to quit because my community inspires me. I see that I am because we are, and I am relentless about pursuing the promise of us.

References

Edwards, F., Lee, H., & Esposito, M. (2019). Risk of being killed by police use of force in the United States by age, race-ethnicity, and sex. *Proceedings of the National Academy of Sciences, 116*(34), 16793-16798.

King, J. E. (Ed.). (2005). *Black education: A transformative research and action agenda for the new century*. Routledge.

Metz, T. (2011). Ubuntu as a moral theory and human rights in South Africa. *African Human Rights Law Journal, 11*(2), 532-559.

Tutu, D. (1999). *No future without forgiveness*. Random House.

We Be Family

It was the end of the school year, and I, Kayla, adjusted Mello's tie for graduation. I had tears in my eyes, trying desperately to hold back my emotions. Mello looked at me and said, "What's wrong, Ma?" I just shook my head and replied, "Nothing." He responded, "I know something is bothering you. What's up?" Sighing, I said, "I am proud of you, but this is a hard day for me. You'll leave here and I won't see you again. I'm just a teacher." He responded, "Nah, we be family." As much as I learned over the 4 years from Mello and his classmates, I missed a critical cultural understanding. I quickly responded, "But, I'm not your real mama. When you come home from college, you will stop and see your real family." Mello just smiled and shook his head. He looked at me and slowly said, "We are family. We were family. We will always be family." Mello is now 24 years old, and he was right. We *be* family. He and his classmates are still my family. We still spend time together, have gatherings, and text often. Teaching students like Mello has been one of the biggest blessings of my life.

Community Building

Black students often experience curricular and instructional violence in schools. As a White female teacher, many Black students and parents enter my room guarded and carrying the trauma of past negative experiences with former teachers. *I, Jamon, experienced many teachers telling me to shut up, be quiet, and stop talking out of turn. I would often be reprimanded for trying to work with my peers. They would tell me I was too loud. I was sent to sit in the hall or kicked out of the classroom, missing the instruction completely. This made me defensive when I would meet new teachers because I had to figure out how they would treat me.* Building a community where students feel comfortable, trusting each other, loved, and respected is my (Kayla's) number one goal.

Décor

Working to build a community begins with focusing on the physical meeting space of the community. I, Kayla, work to make sure that my classroom's physical environment reflects the students I teach and that it has supplies they need to be successful. I make sure to purchase and supply students with novels with main characters that reflect their race and gender readily available in my classroom library. I display these books that show characters that look like them across the room. There are pictures of former students shaped in hearts on the walls. The desks are always set up in three to four groups, so students can work together on all tasks. Every supply that a student could possibly need is at their disposal to use for the entire year. There is a prayer wall dedicated to Tupac—my favorite rapper and poet. There are Adinkra symbols across the top of the whiteboard. After students complete their affirmation flags the first week, their affirmations are posted in the room for the entire year as a reminder to themselves. Our room also has lotion for the students to use at any time and good brands of tissues. There is a snack closet for any student who needs a little nourishment to get through the class. A charging station is set up for their cell phones if they need to charge before they leave for after-school activities or work. I intentionally purchase items for my classroom that will make my students comfortable. I want to show them that I care about their needs as a person, not just the content.

I, Jamon, when first walking into Ms. H's room, was surprised. I never saw a teacher who had a room that looked like hers. My first thoughts were she's different and she must have a thing for Tupac. I saw books that had Black teens on the cover. I noticed that the desks were in groups and all my other teachers had rows. The classroom felt like home. My other classrooms felt like a typical school with the occasional educational posters that said, "If you can dream it, you can do it" or "Deadlines are closer than they appear." I could tell she put some time into her room. Then I found out she had snacks, drinks, and school supplies we could have. She even bought us each our own notebook and folder. I had heard from older students that she was different, but it was another experience to walk into the classroom and see it.

Taking time to make the classroom warm and welcoming for Black students is just one small step to building a community. Classrooms, just like other community spaces, can be set up to show a commitment to social connectedness and to demonstrate love for the whole child or person. See the Guidelines for Community (Table 6.1).

Table 6.1. Guidelines for Community

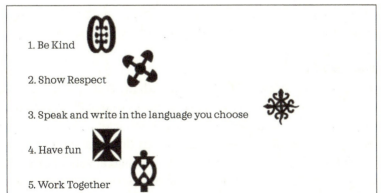

1. Be Kind

2. Show Respect

3. Speak and write in the language you choose

4. Have fun

5. Work Together

The first day of classes at school is boring. Every year is the same routine sitting at a desk and hearing the rules each teacher created. Don't do this, don't do that, if you don't do your work you get a zero. No late work. Ms. H did not do that. She simply put up her guidelines for the community. She said that she did not have a syllabus. Her expectations were as difficult and as simple as the five guidelines she posted. This was a bit shocking to me, Jamon. She moved directly into a story circle.

The guideline that really meant a lot to me was "Speak and write in the language you choose." Ms. H taught us the beauty of using our home languages. She even did some lessons on African American Vernacular. She taught all the kids the rules of the language. I didn't even know the way I talked was considered an official language. I didn't realize it had rules. Ms. H was the only English teacher who never corrected the way I spoke. She never said it was wrong. She let us be us. She showed us how to use Standard English but always gave us a choice in which language we used to turn in assignments. I still wonder how she graded assignments written in Spanish.

Another class guideline that spoke to me was "Work together." We were always permitted to lean on each other for support and help. Ms. H never told us we could not help each other. This was very different from my previous experiences, where I was told to stop talking to my peers. She would often redirect a student to other students for help. She said family helps each other out and trusts in each other. It was a group effort; we rose together.

Oral Traditions

The very first activity I, Kayla, do with my students is a story circle. I explain to the students that every one of them is a storyteller. I tell them that we all have experience listening to and telling stories. In small groups, students take turns telling their story of a bad experience they had at school or with a teacher. After each student shares their entire story, they make a chart of what they had in common. I then ask them to share a story of the good experience they had in school or with a teacher. Again, after each student shares, they make a common list. Then as a class, each group selects a speaker to share the highlights of the stories they heard. We keep a running list of the bad and the good on the whiteboard. Together, as a class community, we create a list of norms and experiences that we want to have for the school year. Throughout, the year I use story circles in different ways. Another example is after reading *All American Boys*, I ask the students to tell a story about an interaction they had with a police officer. Story circles draw on oral traditions and give Black students a space to share their experiences, histories, and truths.

Story circles remind me, Jamon, of talking with my family. They allow everyone to listen and learn from each other. We often laughed a lot when we are doing story circles. They helped us bond, get to know each other, and get comfortable. They also had the power to tell some hard truths. They bring weight to the room sometimes. I remember doing a story circle after reading The Hate U Give *(Thomas, 2017). I was in a group with another Black boy and two White girls. The one White girl's dad was a cop. She told a story about her dad helping a local homeless man. Then it was the other Black boy's turn. He told the story of riding his bike and a cop made him stop. The cop searched him along the road, basically pulled down his pants, and told him he matched a description. His story brought weight to the room. They both spoke their truths, and they were able to gain some new truths from their differences.*

Identity Poetry

Following the story circles, I, Kayla, intentionally plan to build a community with my students through identity poetry and identity assignments. One of the first identity poems that students work on is a "Where I Am From" poem. This poem tells a story about each student's home and some important aspects of their identity. Students share their poems in small groups and have an opportunity to share their poems with the larger group. I, Kayla, always make sure to share my own piece with the students. To show them, I am willing to be vulnerable and share my experiences as well. We create name poems, in which students share the meaning and stories of their names. They write traditional African praise poems, in which students honor an important person in their lives for their skills and/or personality. They write "Raised by Women" poems, in which they honor the people that raised them. They create rings of identity to show the visual rings they bring with them into spaces and deconstruct how they shape their responses. They create affirmations and make a pennant with their affirmations that are displayed all year within the classroom. They share in their small groups and as a large group, taking risks sharing who they are.

The poetry that we created at the beginning of the year and all throughout the year was powerful. It let me, Jamon, tell my story. It helped me show my classmates that there is more to me than what people think. I remember one girl who went to school with me for years and said to me after a week of poetry sharing that she didn't know that I had some challenging experiences. She thought I was just always the happy-go-lucky class clown. It also taught me about my other classmates and showed me I, too, was wrong about some of my perceptions about them. The sharing helped me break down some prejudices I had too.

Text Selections and History

After building a strong community, I, Kayla, intentionally select books that reflect my classroom students. I make sure to include contemporary books and novels such as the following:

- *A Long Way Gone* by Ishmael Beah

- *The Hate U Give* by Angie Thomas

- *Dear Martin* by Nic Stone

- *Things Fall Apart* by Chinua Achebe

- *Purple Hibiscus* by Chimamanda Adichie

- *A Rose That Grew from Concrete* by Tupac

I select these contemporary novels and provide Black students space and time to read about their people's beauty and strength.

The only time I, Jamon, read novels with Black main characters was in Ms. Hostetler's class and in a few elementary classes. In middle school, I did not read one novel that had a Black main character, and in high school, all the other teachers taught boring books about mostly White men. I only learned Black history in school, focusing on two eras, slavery and civil rights history. I never learned Black history pre-enslavement or after the civil rights era or even between the two eras. Ms. H's class was the first time I heard of an Adinkra symbol. I didn't know anything about ancient Africa. I had to teach myself about these topics. I still don't really know how to process my feelings related to this gap in my education. It is hard to understand how so much of Black people's history is left out of textbooks and not taught in history class. As many times as I have learned about slavery and the civil rights era, there was time to learn about ancient Africa.

Speak Up/Stand Up
Through the focus of creating a community, in my, Kayla's, classroom and using African diaspora as the focus of the class's literature, I give students the space to share their truths and begin standing up against inequities. They create

their own literature pieces to share their stories that are often silenced. Their final project for my class is a research project on a social issue they see within their community. They work in groups to conduct a literature review, collect their own data, and develop a plan to act. They also are required to take some sort of action. Through this project, students engage in verve (lively action) and communalism (committing to others).

My, Jamon's, action project changed me. I became empowered and confident in sharing my truth and helping my community. It showed me the power and strength of my community and engaging in community building with others. It helped me understand ubuntu, I am because we are. I started a mentor program in my neighborhood for young Black males, and now I am the youth director of a local youth activist group that I helped form. Ms. H's room became a second home where I grew up.

Mello, Jamon, Nikole, and all my Black students taught me, Kayla, that there is strength and power in unity. Together, we formed a bond that transcended the classroom walls. We built a community and a family. A family that still gathers and helps each other. We practiced and lived and continue to practice an important aspect of African diaspora and culture: communalism. We were, are, and will always be family (see Figures 6.1–6.4).

Figure 6.1. *Nkonsonkonson*: symbol of unity and human relations, a reminder to contribute to the community and that in unity lies strength. *Source:* http://www.adinkra.org/htmls/adinkra/nkon.htm

Figure 6.2. Jamon and Mrs. Hostetler

Figure 6.3. Jamon and Mrs. Hostetler

Figure 6.4. Jamon walking Mrs. Hostetler's daughter to her first basketball game

References

Achebe, C. (1958). *Things fall apart*. William Heinemann Ltd.

Adichie, C. (2003). *Purple hibiscus*. Algonquin Books Kachifo Limited.

Beah, I. (2008). *A long way gone: Memoirs of a boy soldier*. Sarah Crichton.

Shakur, T. (1999). *The rose that grew from concrete*. MTV books.

Stone, N. (2017). *Dear Martin*. Random House Children's Books.

Thomas, A. (2017). *The hate you give*. Balzer & Bray.

Shayla Calhoun and Joy Howard

7

The Crown on Your Head: Teaching African Diaspora Literacy Through Hair

Being Natural is not a statement. It is the closest I can get to being myself.

—Curlyhairlounge.com

Remove the kinks from your mind, not your hair.

—Marcus Garvey

The chapter-opening statements speak to the necessity for hair freedom among Black youth—freedom from judgment, ridicule, and punishment because of hair choices. For far too many Black children in schools, hair has been a site of racialized violence. In response to this reality, we asked ourselves *how teachers (including first teachers [families] and community teachers) rewrite a narrative that affirms natural hair?* Pulling from Gloria Boutte's and her coauthors' (2017) work on African Diaspora Literacies based on A. Wade Boykin's (1983) research on the principles that follow, we put forward three dimensions of African culture as an entry point into this discussion:

- Expressive individualism

- Affect

- Harmony

This chapter highlights examples of conflict over Black hair in recent news, scholarship on the topic, and propositions for creating an inviting space for adults and children to learn about, discuss, and welcome Black hairstyles into various learning spaces.

The Right to Our Hair in Schools: A Brief Overview

Devastating disparities in school discipline have been noted and discussed all over the country (Alexander, 2012; Blad & Harwin, 2017). Too often, Black students are punished for "violating" subjective school dress code policies, specifically related to hairstyles. Black students have been scrutinized for their head coverings and hairstyles, signifying natural and cultural norms:

- High school senior, Lawrence Charles, was suspended for wearing his du-rag to school (*The Grio*, 2018).

- Wrestler Andrew Johnson was forced to cut off his dreadlocks during a wrestling match (Blackistone, 2018).

- Six-year-old Clinton Stanley Jr. was sent home from his first day of school because of his dreadlocks (Morgan-Smith, 2018).

- Thirteen-year-old J. T.'s teacher colored his hair with a black marker (Sparks, 2019), and 8-year-old Marian Scott was excluded from school pictures because of her new red hair extensions (Alsharif, 2019).

- Pictures featuring Black hairstyles at Narvie J. Harris Elementary School in Decatur, Georgia, demonstrated what *not* to wear to school (Vigdor, 2019).

Attacks on Black children's bodies, minds, and spirits occur every day. Black students' hair is not a problem to be fixed or managed. Colonizing and oppressive messages embedded in Eurocratic practices and policies must be changed (King and Swartz, 2015). Punishing Black students for their hairstyles and head covering choices is both demeaning and exclusionary. These practices and policies violate children's rights to an education, and change is necessary.

Connecting to a Broader Conversation

Hair has always been an integral part of African American culture and identity, with deep African roots that existed before slavery (Brooks & McNair, 2015; Byrd & Tharps, 2001). Hair care and styles are an important part of bonding and building relationships with the community. Discussions about hair in the school curriculum are essential to all students' well-being, especially Black students. A promising move toward justice is the CROWN Act (Creating a Respectful and Open Workplace for Natural Hair), which began in January 2020, to eliminate institutional biases based on discrimination against natural hair (Blaes & Domek, 2019).

The Call for Teachers and Youth Workers to Do Better

Educators must reflect on Black hair as a cultural expression site, a human right, and a strength. Educators must work toward practices that invite students to be fully engaged as a part of the learning community. This includes their hair. Children's experiences with their hair, whether positive or negative, will influence how they see themselves and the world around them. Black children need to be exposed to literary works that feature characters that look like them because it shapes how they view the world and themselves. Understanding the significance of hair in literary works is essential because of hair matters (Brooks & McNair, 2015; Edwards, 2005).

To confront the damaging messages in society, as a whole, and school spaces, specifically, we must build on Black culture's strengths as we teach and learn. The Adinkra symbol *duafe*—the wooden comb, which symbolizes beauty and cleanliness or looking at one's best (see Figure 7.1)—is a value expressed in West African culture. We take up this symbol to indicate the cultural emphasis on hairstyles as integral for defining beauty from an Afrocentric perspective. Building on this concept, we focus on several African principles to inform curriculum and teaching relative to Black hair in learning spaces: expressive individualism, affect, and harmony.

Figure 7.1. Duafe—"wooden comb"—a symbol of beauty and cleanliness representing looking one's best
Source: http://www.adinkra.org/htmls/adinkra/duafe.htm

Boutte and coauthors (2017) explain *expressive individualism* as the cultivation of a distinctive personality and proclivity for spontaneous and genuine personal expression. *Affect* emphasizes emotions and feelings and sensitivity to emotional cues and the tendency to be emotionally expressive. *Harmony* refers to the notion that one's fare is interrelated with other elements in the scheme of things so that humankind and nature are harmonically conjoined. We apply these African principles to real-life examples of how each of these dimensions has come to life in Shayla's classroom.

Our Connections With Black Hair

Shayla

I am an African American elementary school teacher, graduate student, and parent of four children. I have taught for more than 10 years in kindergarten through third grade and worked extensively with many fourth- and fifth-grade students through after-school extracurricular activities such as basketball and our school's step team. As I am a parent with four children, hair is very much a part of my life. My exploration of Black hair in the classroom began in 2018. I made two major life changes. I made the decision to go natural and to start a doctoral program in educational leadership. This was a pivotal moment in my personal and professional journey. In my returning natural journey, I realized that returning my hair to its natural state was much deeper than I had ever perceived. It caused me to evaluate who I am and what defines me as an individual, which led me to where I am now exploring natural hair in an educational setting.

Joy

My exploration of Black hair in the classroom has grown out of three sources of inspiration. As a White mother scholar (Howard et al., in press), my scholarly interests are intimately connected to my role as the mother of three Black mixed-race sons. I have observed and mediated some of their experiences inside and outside of schools where hair has been a primary entry point for how people see my children racially (e.g., strangers stating, "Wow, his hair is curly. Can I touch it? What is he?") and how they express themselves racially (e.g., one of my sons decided to get cornrows before entering a new school to assert his African ancestry). My ongoing work about Black mixed-race children's experiences in schools (Howard, 2019) affirmed hair as a primary symbol that teachers, students, and the school community use to ascribe race to Black mixed-race students. Shayla's inquiry about Black hair was fascinating to me as a mother, learner, instructor, and advisor. We describe how Shayla has applied three key principles: expressive individualism, affect, and harmony by intentionally affirming Black hair in the classroom.

African Principles in the Curriculum

Expressive Individualism

As a facilitator, I encourage students to see themselves not just as individuals but as amazing individuals. When I did the "big chop," I had to reimagine my hair. I had to figure out what to do with it. I had to get accustomed to wearing and creating new hairstyles such as pineapples, buns, and free curls. I noticed that my students and other teachers saw me differently. Some students seemed to admire my hair while others appeared confused and expressed their confusion. I began to question my beauty and uniqueness, but about 9 months into the transition, I decided that I would love my natural hair.

Expressive individualism, the cultivation of a distinctive personality and genuine personal expression is demonstrated in the book *I Love My Hair* by Natasha Anastasia Tarpley (2003). The book tells a story about the importance of loving your hair because it is your hair. I ask children to create portraits of themselves and use descriptive adjectives (e.g., curly) to complete a writing assignment. In a classroom setting or community space, expressive individualism begins when students are free to show who they are as individuals. Making connections to art and history, having open discussions about the process of braiding or experiences at barbershops, or featuring literature that displays unique styles would all support a celebration of expressive individualism.

Improvisation

Improvisation includes the substitution of alternatives that are more sensitive to Black culture. Exposing students to various narratives allows them to see elements of themselves through the characters and people they read about. Most students know about or have read some version of "Goldilocks and the Three Bears," but Yolanda King's (2015), *Curlilocks and the Big Bad Hairbrush* is a version told through the lens of a curly-haired Brown-skinned girl. Books that reflect the students I teach increase students' confidence. Stories like this one can teach a variety of skills and concepts such as central message, comparing and contrasting, creative writing, or as part of a book study exploring different versions of "Goldilocks and the Three Bears." Students can work in small groups using props and other materials to retell the story while identifying the characters, setting, and other important key details or to use a reader's theater format. One year, my students wrote their own version and performed it for their families at school—creating their own background props and making a dessert. Students and teachers at the school were also invited to attend. Reflecting on this event made me realize the importance of improvisation and the necessity to be more attuned to Black culture. Allowing Black students to star as themselves with their natural hairstyles can greatly impact their self-esteem.

Affect

Affect emphasizes emotions and feelings and sensitivity to emotional cues as well as the tendency to be emotionally expressive. As a Black educator, who has natural hair, I have become highly sensitive to my students' feelings and emotional cues. I have noticed students who have tried to hide or avoid classmates because they have been ashamed of their hair, such as students hiding in the bathroom or repeatedly going to the bathroom to style their hair or trying to cover up their natural locks.

The struggle to get your hair just right can be paralyzing. These experiences made me realize that appearance is very important to children, including how their hair looks. I have begun to reflect on my memories as a child, and my own current hair experiences, and as a mother of two girls and two boys with natural hair. I have realized that my experiences were not just my own. This gives me a sense of pride in who I am as an educator and the diverse skill set I bring to the table. Books that support affect include *I Am Enough!* by Grace Byers (2018), and *I Like Myself!* by Karen Beaumont (2010). Students can reflect on themes of self-esteem, empathy, respect, and celebrating uniqueness in reading responses. I have had students write and share what makes them unique. Prompting students with sentence starters, such as *If I could describe myself using three words . . . , I am unique because . . . ,* and *I like myself because . . .* , can help them conceptualize their thoughts. Educators must be aware of the effects—of the emotions, feelings, and needs of Black students.

Harmony

Students should be actively engaged in and considered while planning instructional content. The inclusion of children of all races with a common goal in mind (harmony) is essential. Texts must be carefully selected and activities must be intentional. If students can't envision themselves or relate to a literature piece, then harmony is not achieved. Harmony in a classroom setting could include students using the following books to write their own unique stories, write or draw what harmony looks like in their own communities, and explain responsibilities as a group or community member:

- *One Love* (Marley, 2014)

- *Hair Love* (Cherry, 2019)

- *Don't Touch My Hair* (Miller, 2019). Students can discuss the importance of respecting others' possessions, including hair.

Conclusion

We hope that readers can envision themselves as catalysts to change the narrative about Black hair by acknowledging that this narrative includes everyone—Black and non-Black natural hair. We encourage readers to adapt these examples to unique teaching and learning contexts and expand on these dimensions to affirm Black children's strength and beauty, including their hair, in our community, educational, and home spaces.

References

Alexander, M. (2012). *The new Jim Crow: Mass incarceration in the age of colorblindness*. The New Press.

Alsharif, M. (2019, November 20). *Michigan 8-year-old gets photo shoot after being denied school picture for her hair extensions*. CNN. https://www.cnn.com/2019/11/19/us/michigan-8-year-old-photo-shoot-trnd/index.html

Beaumont, K. (2010). *I like myself!* HMH Books for Young Readers.

Blackistone, K. B. (2018, December 28). *Wrestler being forced to cut dreadlocks was manifestation of decades of racial desensitization*. Washington Post. https://www.washingtonpost.com/sports/wrestler-being-forced-to-cut-dreadlocks-was-manifestation-of-decades-of-racial-desensitization/2018/12/27/66f520ba-0a10-11e9-85b6-41c0fe0c5b8f_story.html?noredirect=on&utm_term=.a1eb2bc98c06

Blad, E., & Harwin, A. (2017). Black students more likely to be arrested at school. Policing America's schools. *Education Week, 36*(19), 1-12.

Blaes, L. J., & Domek, N. L. (2019, August 22). *A heads up on the CROWN Act: Employees' natural hairstyles now protected*. The National Law Review. https://www.natlawreview.com/article/heads-crown-act-employees-natural-hairstyles-now-protected

Boutte, G. S., Johnson, G. L., Wynter-Hoyt, K., & Uyoata, U. E. (2017). Using African Diaspora Literacy to heal and restore the souls of Black folks. *International Critical Childhood Policy Studies Journal, 6*(1), 66–79.

Boykin, A. W. (1983). The academic performance of Afro-American children. In J. Spence (Ed.), *Achievement and achievement motives* (pp. 323–371). Freeman.

Brooks, W. M., & McNair, J. C. (2015). "Combing" through representations of black girls' hair in African American children's literature. *Gender and Education, 46*(3), 296–307. http://doi10.1080/09540253.2016.12 21888

Byers, G. (2018). *I am enough*. Balzer & Bray Publishing.

Byrd, A. & Tharps, L. (2001). *Hair story: Untangling the roots of Black hair in America*. St. Martin's Press.

Calhoun, S. (2020). *The crown on your head: Teaching African diaspora literacy through hair* [Unpublished manuscript]. University of Southern Indiana.

Cherry, M. A. (2019). *Hair love*. Kokila.

Edwards, D. (2005, Spring). "Doing hair" and literacy in an afterschool reading and writing workshop for African American adolescent girls. *Afterschool Matters*, (4), 42–50.

The Grio. (2018, April 20). *Arizona high schooler suspended for wearing durag says his punishment is racist*. https://thegrio.com/2018/04/20/arizona-principal-suspends-student-durag/

Howard, J. (2019). Just playin': Multiracial boys and the injustice of boyhood. *Race Ethnicity and Education*. Advanced online publication. https://doi.org/10.1080/13613324.2019.1679760

Howard, J., Thompson, C., & Nash, K. (In press). Mother (space) Scholar (space): Poetic inquiries of motherscholaring. *Qualitative Studies in Education*.

King, J. E., & Swartz, E. E. (2015). *The Afrocentric praxis of teaching for freedom: Connecting culture to learning.* Routledge.

King, Y. (2015). *Curlilocks and the big bad hairbrush.* Tangled Press.

Marley, C. (2014). *One love.* Chronicle Books.

Miller, S. (2019). *Don't touch my hair.* Little, Brown Books for Readers.

Morgan-Smith, K. (2018, August 16). *Adorable six-year-old boy banned from school for dreadlocks.* The Grio. https://thegrio.com/2018/08/16/adorable-six-year-old-black-boy-banned-from-school-for-dreadlocks/

Sparks, H. (2019, August 20). *School forced Black student to "Sharpie in" his haircut: Lawsuit.* New York Post. https://nypost.com/2019/08/20/school-forced-black-student-to-sharpie-in-his-haircut-lawsuit/

Tarpley, N. A. (2003). *I love my hair.* LB Kids.

Vigdor, N. (2019, August 3). *Georgia elementary school is accused of racial insensitivity over hairstyle guidelines display.* New York Times. https://www.nytimes.com/2019/08/03/us/hairstyles-black-students-appropriate-inappropriate.html

8

Lasana D. Kazembe, Leslie K. Etienne, and Tambra O. Jackson

Teaching Our Children About Blackness in the World

In 2006, *National Geographic* issued a famous survey to measure geographic literacy rates among young adults worldwide. Sadly, the lack of global knowledge (e.g., recognizing names and locations of countries, continents, bodies of water) remains a serious problem—especially among U.S. students. Geographic literacy (referred to as *geoliteracy*) describes the multiple ways in which people understand, interpret, and interact with the world. When students possess geoliteracy skills, they can also better assess themselves and their place in the world. When geoliteracy is incorporated into education, students (especially younger children) benefit by gaining a deeper understanding of

- world cultures and historically significant events,

- diverse ways of learning and interacting with content, and

- interconnections across multiple diverse areas of culture (e.g., arts, cuisine, language).

For Black children, geoliteracy is especially important because of its potential to expand and deepen (particularly within community learning spaces) their knowledge of history and culture. Liberatory Black community learning spaces in the United States (e.g., African Free Schools, Citizenship Schools, Freedom Schools, Sabbath Schools, Midnight Schools) have played an important role and have a proud legacy of learning and resilience outside of formal school. In this chapter, we describe two educational programs: Freedom Schools and elev8te. Specifically, we discuss how each is focused on the African diaspora and enacted within extracurricular contexts.

Figure 8.1. *Nea onnim no sua a ohu*—"one who does not know can know from learning" (knowledge, lifelong education and continued quest for knowledge)
Source: http://www.adinkra.org/htmls/adinkra/neao.htm

The African diaspora refers to people of African origin who live outside of the African continent and who are spread throughout the world. Here are a few population estimates of people of African ancestry in the diaspora:

- North America: 39 million

- Latin America: 113 million

- Caribbean: 14 million

- Europe: 3.5 million

Those big numbers include large groups of Africans located throughout French Guiana, Colombia, Dominica, as well as Lisbon. Now, if those faraway places seem totally unfamiliar to you, then you are not alone. One of the basic goals of geoliteracy, to make the unfamiliar familiar, affirms the cultural principle of the nea onnim no sua a ohu, the Adinkra symbol shown in Figure 8.1, to engage in a continued quest for knowledge.

When it comes to educating Black youth, we must locate and develop creative ways to keep them engaged. Black youth must understand the world around them and how people and ideas are interconnected. Geoliteracy is crucial because it enhances Black youth's preparedness to acquire a deeper understanding of cultures and enhanced reasoning skills within and across learning contexts. It provides a gateway for positive Black student learning breakthroughs.

Collectively, Freedom Schools and elev8te represent powerful models for deepening and enriching Black children and youth's education. For example, there is value for African American students to be engaged in deep learning about the living legacy of Ella Baker and the history and impact of the Tuskegee model. Similarly, there is value in African American students learning about how Haitian artists created a literary and artistic movement that challenged racism and global imperialism. As we reveal, there are lots of rich, fascinating connections and interconnections within and across both contexts.

Figure 8.2. *mate masie*—"What I hear, I keep" (wisdom, knowledge, prudence)
Source: http://www.adinkra.org/htmls/adinkra/mate.htm

Geoliteracy and Freedom Schools

Literacy and education for liberation have always been important themes within Black community spaces. The Freedom

School model was designed to transform communities by helping people to recognize their collective strengths and to exercise their political power. In this sense, the Freedom School concept aligns with the mate masie Adinkra symbol shown in Figure 8.2, emphasizing the importance of internalizing knowledge. In the modern context, Freedom Schools serve the vital function of emphasizing the connection between education and freedom. Annually, tens of thousands of students (referred to as scholars in the program) participate in Freedom Schools sponsored by schools, churches, and nonprofit organizations. These scholars are routinely introduced to literature and learning, highlighting how Black people have used education to pursue freedom.

They Learned Under the Trees

Freedom Schools emerged during the era of the 1960s' Black Freedom movement. They were temporary schools that offered Black children supplemental learning and emboldened young people critically to question the world in which they lived. A distinctive aspect of Freedom Schools was their resistance to racist schooling systems that went to great lengths to maintain the status quo and worked to keep Black students down. The Black students who attended the different variations of Freedoms Schools were unbowed. They learned under trees, in makeshift community centers, and in church basements. They could be found in locations such as the Arkansas Delta; the Mississippi Delta; Boston; Selma, Alabama; and Farmville, Virginia. Freedom Schools are a historical but sometimes forgotten testament to emancipatory Black Education. One of the most identifiable Freedom Schools examples can be found during the 1964 Mississippi Summer Project (also known as the Freedom Summer), the Student Nonviolent Coordinating Committee (SNCC), and other civil rights organizations enacted.

Freedom Summer not only still stands as one of the pivotal moments in breaking through well-entrenched racism but also provides a glaring model for what can happen when local people and, more importantly, youth engage in mass organizing. The SNCC Freedom Schools curriculum and structure as a model for Black children's emancipatory education is a redemptive feature of the Black Freedom movement that is still relevant today.

I can make a difference in my world.

The Children's Defense Fund (CDF) Freedom Schools are a contemporary reiteration of the 1964 Freedom Schools. The program is focused on literacy, civic engagement, and social action, and the curriculum spans kindergarten through 12th grade. The overarching theme of the CDF Freedom Schools curriculum is "I Can Make a Difference." Each week of the program focuses on six subthemes that allow youth participants to explore their ability to make a difference in self, family, community, country, world, and hope, education, and action. Within the Freedom Schools curriculum, geoliteracy is most visible in the subtheme of "I Can Make a Difference in My World." The subtheme's goal for making a difference in the world is to help scholars explore the world and how their stories connect with others around the globe. Stories about African people and culture around the world are explored through books such as the following:

- *Anansi the Spider: A Tale from the Ashanti* (McDermott, 1972)

- *Beatrice's Goat* (McBrier, 2001)

- *Desmond and the Very Mean Word* (Tutu & Abrams, 2013)

- *I and I: Bob Marley* (Medina, 2009)

- *Masai and I* (Kroll, 1992)

- *The Girl Who Buried Her Dreams in a Can: A True Story* (Trent, 2015)

- *Tutankhamen's Gift* (Sabuda, 1994)

- *14 Cows for America* (Deedy, 2009)

Alongside reading the books, students are engaged in cooperative learning activities such as role-playing, poetry, artwork, graphic organizers, social action, and conflict resolution that bring the stories to life. This approach is intended to help the scholars keep the diaspora's wisdom and knowledge beyond their summer in the program.

Figure 8.3. *Nsaa*—one who does not know authentic nsaa (cloths) will buy fakes (meaning: excellence, genuineness, authenticity) *Source:* http://www.adinkra.org/htmls/adinkra/nsaa.htm

Geoliteracy and Global Black Arts Movements
Despite the serious need, very little learning about the arts and world geography is offered to Black students in U.S. schools. Research on culturally informed understanding has shown that regular and consistent exposure to cultural arts learning opportunities has a profound positive impact on students. Education researchers have identified five important elements of culturally responsive education:

- Cultural literacy

- Self-reflective analysis of one's beliefs

- Caring

- Trusting and inclusive classrooms, respect for diversity

- A transformative curriculum

These five elements reflect excellence and authenticity individually and collectively, the cultural meanings connected to the nsaa Adinkra symbol shown in Figure 8.3. Next, we reflect on (1) experiences from an afterschool literacy and creative arts curriculum and program that Professor Kazembe created and (2) the role of geoliteracy within the curriculum and the facilitation.

Using Global Black Arts Movements to Elevate Black Children's Learning

elev8te is a literacy and creative arts program that introduces participants to the cultural, historical, and political impact of the six Global Black Arts Movements mentioned later. Explicitly designed for elementary school-age students, elev8te introduces them to a nearly century-long tradition of Black arts and artists (i.e., writers, poets, visual and performing artists) who developed and used art to transform themselves and society. The program introduces Black students to culturally and historically significant art, music, and literature developed within the Global Black Arts Movements.

Spanning nearly a century, Global Black Arts Movements represented an exciting Black creative expression and cultural development period. During the 20th century, Black writers, poets, visual, and performing artists established six crucial historical, social, and cultural movements that flourished in the United States, Europe, Africa, and the Caribbean. Known as *Global Black Arts Movements*, they included the following:

- Indigéniste (Haiti)

- Négrismo (Cuba and Puerto Rico)

- Négritude (Paris, French Guiana, Martinique)

- New Negro Movement/Harlem Renaissance (New York)

- Black Chicago Renaissance (Chicago)

- Black Arts Movement (United States)

Global Black Arts Movements linked Black artists-activists in international campaigns for freedom and liberation. Black intellectuals and artists developed and used art to mount campaigns of resistance, social justice, education, and cultural expression.

Geoliteracy is an important component of the elev8te program. During the first segment of the six-part program, students learn about Indigéniste, the artistic movement developed in Haiti during the 1920s and 1930s. Haitian writers, artists, and activists of that period understood the word *Indigéniste* as referring to their search for their *Blackness or African identity*. Students can make an immediate, authentic connection between the search for identity among Haitians and African Americans. As students learn about the writers and activists who developed the Indigéniste movement, they also study maps and country history. During this component of the program, students learn about Haiti's physical location and its proximity and importance to other areas of the African diaspora.

Geoliteracy is further emphasized in the students' learning about the poetry/poets/poetics of the Global Black Arts Movements. For example, as students read poetry from the Négrismo movement (the artistic and social movement that evolved in Cuba and Puerto Rico during the 1920s), they learn how to pronounce and identify geoliteracy sight words and cultural terms such as *peasant, fiesta,* and *El Morro*. When students encounter these words, they are automatically linked to a particular place in the world (Cuba or Puerto Rico), a particular era (the postcolonial period), and a particular people (Afro-Cubans). Additionally, teaching geoliteracy skills enables students to make an instant connection to particular historical/political contexts (e.g., the struggle against enslavement and imperialism; the search for and celebration of African identity and Black cultural expression).

When students develop geoliteracy skills, they become more globally connected, informed, and active. Geoliteracy provides a gateway for students to acquire the deep learning and robust skills that are so critical in today's world.

Figure 8.4. *akoma ntoso*—"linked hearts" (agreement and understanding)
Source: http://www.adinkra.org/htmls/adinkra/akon.htm

Conclusion

When the cultural meaning of the akoma ntoso (see Figure 8.4) is activated, we all benefit from mutual agreement and understanding. We have discussed two different education programs (Freedom Schools and elev8te) and described how each contributes to enriching and expanding Black students' educational possibilities. Geoliteracy is an important feature of both curricula as it is designed to challenge and enhance the way students understand and see the world. By expanding their understanding of *where* African people are, students understand *who* African people are. Geoliteracy is crucial to Black students' education because it encourages them to develop a broader lens on African people's culture, experiences, and shared history throughout the world. In turn, this expanded view allows Black students to gain insight and inspiration by studying and seeing the deep cultural interconnections among and between people sprinkled throughout the African diaspora.

With the police murder of George Floyd in Minneapolis during the summer of 2020, we entered a new phase of racial protest uprising and struggle for liberation. One of the key questions that continues to be raised is "What do we tell our children?" For long decades, Freedom Schools have functioned as sites of community discourse and models for education, democratic engagement, and community transformation. Those who create, teach in, and support Freedom Schools regard them as important vehicles for Black children and youth's education.

The optimal and holistic development of Black children is a prominent feature within and across both models that we have discussed. Within these alternative learning settings, Black students engage in rich discussions and learning experiences about identity, power, culture, and history. Unlike traditional educational contexts, the Freedom Schools and elev8te models provide students with a strong foundation and context to understand difficult subjects such as racial violence, imperialism, and colonization. Both models emphasize the resilience, heritage, and enormous diversity of African ancestry people both in the United States and throughout the world.

References

Deedy, C. A. (2009). *14 cows for America*. Peachtree Publishing Company.

Kroll, V. (1992). *Masai and I*. Aladdin.

McBrier, P. (2004). *Beatrice's goat*. Aladdin.

McDermott, G. (1972). *Anansi the spider: A tale from the Ashanti*. Henry Holt & Company.

Medina, T. (2009). *I and I: Bob Marley*. Lee & Low Books.

Sabuda, R. (1994). *Tutankhamen's gift*. Aladdin.

Trent, T. (2015). *The girl who buried her dreams in a can: A true story*. Viking Books for Young Readers.

Tutu, D., & Abrams, D. C. (2012). *Desmond and the very mean word*. Candlewick Press.

 Part II

BLACK FOLKS ALL OVER THE WORLD

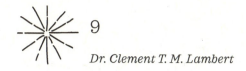

African Diaspora Literacy in Jamaica and the Wider Caribbean

Jamaica: An Introduction

Nestled in the Western Caribbean between Cuba and Hispaniola is Jamaica—the largest English-speaking nation in the Caribbean. With a population of under 3 million, about 92% of the residents are of African descent. Jamaica is famous for reggae music (Bob Marley), athletics (Usain Bolt), and pioneering intellectual thought on pan-Africanism (Marcus Garvey). Despite the rich heritage that runs deep in the Jamaican vein, it is a country of paradoxes and controversies related to African diaspora literacy.

Imagine an island of a little over 4,000 square miles with lush landscapes. Hills, valleys, plains, mountains, and beautiful beaches are all within an hour's ride. A country with rich religious roots as well as a voracious appetite for revelry, the unique cuisine is deeply influenced by African, European, and Asian ingredients and techniques. Jamaica is a country where politics and policies have shaped national development and the will of its people. The country's motto is "out of many one people," yet the Indigenous populations were totally decimated by European colonizers, and the European slave trade provided African slaves for centuries. Imagine a country trying to break from the colonial legacies that entailed brutality and prejudice but produced some of the most persistent and creative minds. Yes, you have imagined Jamaica—a country where Europeans first arrived in 1494 that Columbus described as the most beautiful isle he had ever seen. Like its Caribbean counterparts, when cane sugar was in its heyday Jamaica was the breadbasket for European colonizers. The actions of the colonizers shaped both the population and the economy of these islands for centuries. The colonial legacy of Jamaica includes genocide, slavery, and bloody slave revolts. Yet the official head of state of Jamaica is still Queen Elizabeth, and the country still boasts a Westminster-style government. Despite the colonial legacy of oppression and abuse, Jamaica's heritage also includes stories of creativity, unbridled talent, resistance, and triumph. One striking example is in the stories of Nanny of the Maroons—Jamaica's only national heroine who holds legendary status for her tactical triumphs over a well-equipped British army. Nanny, a famous Maroon warrior leader, fought across the "New World," including in South America, the United States, and the Caribbean. She is known for resistance to slavery via uprisings (Brown, 2020).

Schooling in Jamaica

Schooling and teaching in Jamaica began even before slavery ended in 1838. Enslavers' children typically went back to England to study. Some Jamaicans who were enslaved learned to read based on their status as "house slaves" and their interactions with their "masters." Others were taught to read by missionaries under the guise of converting them to Christianity. After slavery ended, many former slaves did not want to be connected with the memories of their forced and harsh work on sugar plantations. Despite their best efforts to resist, slavery and negative race relations have lingered in the Jamaican psyche for a long time.

Education became a very attractive pathway away from that route. Schools started through trust funds, churches, and eventually, the government began to educate the general population. Today, the education system has evolved in Jamaica, where universal education is mostly government-funded for children from kindergarten to 11th grade. The curriculum is government-designed and highly influenced by high-stakes examinations at various stages of schooling. Despite catering to over 90% of students from the African diaspora, this curriculum has little direct reference to African heritage, and teachers are not formally prepared to promote African diaspora literacy in schools.

Jamaican Perspectives

Jamaica often presents as the story of two countries. Kingston, the capital, was declared a cultural site by the United Nations in 2019. This honor was given because of many famous Jamaicans (including Bob Marley) and their contributions to the international cultural landscape. During apartheid in South Africa, Jamaican entertainers and even politicians were among the most vocal calling for an end to apartheid through song (e.g., "Free Mandela," "Can You?" among many others),[1] speeches, and boycotts. The Rastafarian religion, which emerged in Jamaica, had strong African perspectives and a very vocal "back to Africa" message. The Universal Negro Improvement Association, founded by Marcus Garvey, heralded the theme "Africa for Africans at home and abroad," also a strong back-to-Africa theme.

The "second" Jamaica entailed a rigid school system and policymakers who rejected the native Jamaican language (which has gone through several names—Patois, Jamaican Creole, and now Jamaican). The official language of instruction

---

1   Many more songs can be located by a simple Google search on Jamaican anti-apartheid songs.

is English, and Jamaican talk has only recently (around 2000) been acknowledged as the home language of over 90% of the children who attend schools. Jamaican, which is a combination of African and European languages, was designated as "bad talk" by educators and policymakers. Therefore, it lacked the sponsorship to be formalized as a language of instruction for Jamaican students. Jamaican creole is the dominant mode of communication for the mass of the people in the Caribbean (Bryan, 2010). Bryan cites a very heavy Twi (a dialect of the Akan language spoken mostly in south and central Ghana; "Twi," 2000) influence on the pronunciation, grammar, and vocabulary of the Jamaican language. She explains that Jamaican language also has roots in many different European and even Asian languages. Perhaps her most striking observation is that

> the most significant non-British category is the African. The African lexicon is significant and is used in all aspects of life but is especially numerous in plants, foods, utensils, music, dancing, superstition, people and their conditions, and greetings and exclamations. . . . A few examples include: ackee, pumpun, afu, yampee (plants); duckunu, janga, toto, busu (food); bankra, cotta (furnishings/utensils); ketta, abeng (music); jumbi, obeah (beliefs); bafan, yaw (ailments) . . . (Bryan, 2010, p. 11)

The work of cultural activists has also promoted the importance of Jamaican language and its linkages to our African roots. Louise Bennett ("Miss Lou"—a cultural icon) is very important in prompting and legitimizing Jamaican talk. Bennett was a Jamaican poet, performer and cultural ambassador who pioneered the promotion of the Jamaican language in significant ways (Cooper, 2009).

Color has also been a dominant issue in Jamaica. While this has evolved, historically, a person of lighter complexion is more favorably considered in many circles. They had a better chance of being selected for certain jobs and even better relationships and marriage choices. This and other factors have led to the neglect of African heritage in formal and informal circles and to issues such as rampant skin bleaching. These factors have long pointed to the need for African diaspora literacy among the Jamaican population.

The Jamaican School Curriculum

The Jamaican school curriculum covers a wide range of subjects and tracks for school completion. In our primary schools (Grades 1-6), English language arts, mathematics, science, social studies, religious education, health and family life education, and civics, to a lesser extent, are included in the curriculum. A close examination of the Jamaican curriculum revealed references to the Jamaican heritage, but very little reference is made to Africa and our African heritage.

Teacher preparation (preservice and in-service) has not formally contributed to teacher awareness of or inclusion of African diaspora literacy in their instruction. I interviewed teachers from elementary schools across Jamaica, and they candidly described a situation that pointed to the need for African diaspora literacy for students, parents, and themselves as teachers. The teachers were candid in stating the term *African diaspora literacy* was very new to them. According to one teacher I call Terrylee,[2]

> Well, I have never heard it before but let me unpack it to see if I am on the right track. African diaspora refers to persons of African descent around the world. Literacy what I am looking at is it based on an Afrocentric perspective based on your understanding of your heritage and history.

---

2 Pseudonyms are used to protect the teachers' identity.

Denise, another teacher, stated,

> It means maybe like different African groups. . . . Maybe
> different African groups of people live in other coun-
> tries—so their literacy is like learning about their cul-
> tural background.

The teachers quoted made good inferences regarding what
African diaspora literacy might be. However, others offer-
ed erroneous explanations, including "the literacy rate of
Africans."

Whatever definitions the Jamaican teachers gave regarding African diaspora literacy, our conversations pointed to
the negative effects of Western education and perspectives
and the need for a greater celebration of our African identity
in Jamaican schools. According to Terrylee,

> I've been teaching for 12 years, and I've yet to see there's
> been just talk about integrating our history (more so the
> teachings of Marcus Garvey) in schools. It was done in the
> past, but for decades now, that has been tossed aside. So,
> every year we turn out students who are inundated with
> Americanized culture. And the aspects of that culture that
> are celebrated are not the aspects that speak to self-love as
> persons of African descent.

Denise poignantly points to the effects of Western perspectives which transcends student education and points to a pro-
foundly rooted situation:

> Some of us as teachers are kind of enslaved, too, because as
> adults, some believe that if our nose no strait, we not pretty.
> We have to change our mindset as well to find importance
> in teaching those students. Because even though we talk

about it and we say we should love our Blackness and whatever, you have some persons you go on the road, and you see persons of dark complexion. We exclaim at his Blackness and often equate Blackness with ugliness. But if we see a White person, we say, "Wow she is so pretty!" ... If our mindset is changed, even if it is not a part of the curriculum, we can do things that children will emulate to see, you know, praise Black people. When you have the little Black children at home, compliment their complexion instead of saying, "How you so Black, gal?"

Effect of Western Education on Jamaican Children

Jamaica has mostly followed a Western model of education, which has left deeply rooted implicit and explicit Western values in Jamaican children's perspectives. Traditionally, the curriculum lauded European "pioneers" who "discovered" Jamaica and benevolent Europeans who saw to our freedom. This has changed to a more balanced perspective over the years. However, what has not received enough attention in the formal education system is the systematic exploration of our African heritage and promoting value and pride in this dimension that accounts for the heritage of the wider Jamaican and Caribbean populations. Unfortunately, being "too Black" is still perceived as a disadvantage in some Jamaican circles. This can be attributed to the centuries of projecting Eurocentric images in education and religious literature. While the tides are changing, Western education has disproportionately favored stories of European triumph and downplayed African greatness. Marcus Garvey recognized this anomaly almost a century ago when he declared, "A **people without** the knowledge of their past history, origin and culture is like a tree **without** roots" (Afrobella, 2009, emphasis added). This underscores the need for African diaspora literacy then and even more so now. To promote awareness and appreciation of self it is important to include cultural knowledge (i.e., African history, religion, science, and philosophy) in the Jamaican school curriculum.

Recommendation for Families and Communities in Jamaica and the Caribbean

The formal school system has been moving too slowly toward promoting African diaspora literacy in Jamaica and the Caribbean. Therefore, parents and families need to take steps to enable this essential dimension as discussed in the following recommendations.

Public Awareness, Buy-In, and Advocacy

There are pockets in the Jamaican population that have valued and continue to promote our African heritage—not necessarily in the name of African diaspora literacy. The Bobo Ashanti community of Bull Bay ("Bobo Ashanti," 2020) and Liberty Hall, established by Marcus Garvey and evolved into a center for teaching and celebrating matters pertinent to the African diaspora (Williams, 2019), are notable examples. However, these communities tend to be under-recognized within Jamaican education circles. Alliances between notable scholars (e.g., Boutte et al., 2017, 2018) and Jamaican advocates would add legitimacy to promoting African diaspora literacy in the Caribbean.

Caribbean families and communities can be instrumental in advocacy by lobbying local schools and governments through parent-teacher associations, media appearances, and other means to place greater emphasis on African diaspora literacy in schools.

Increasing Knowledge of African Diaspora Literacy

Caribbean families and communities need to know the importance of African diaspora literacy through essential readings, public lectures, and exploration of websites. Even a search of local newspapers on the topic might be useful. It is also essential to explore history books (e.g., Diptee, 2010) that provide a more balanced view of the transatlantic journey of Africans to the Western Hemisphere. Jamaica and the wider Caribbean are on a quest to balance and further understand their intellectual, social, and cultural heritage. Greater attention to African diaspora literacy will prove to be an essential dimension of this journey.

Internet Resources

- O'Gilvie, D. (n.d.). *Ghana and Nigeria: Jamaica's not-so-distant relatives*. http://www.griotsrepublic.com/ghana-nigeria-jamaicas-not-distant-relatives/

- Editorial Team. (2020, June 27). *History of Jamaica*. B:M20. https://www.blackhistorymonth.org.uk/article/section/jamaica/history-of-jamaica/

- Charles, C. A. D. (2003). Skin bleaching, self-hate and Black Identity in Jamaica. *Journal of Black Studies, 33*(6), 711–728. https://citeseerx.ist.psu.edu/viewdoc/download?doi=10.1.1.895.8713&rep=rep1&type=pdf

- National Standards Curriculum of Jamaica:

  https://pep.moey.gov.jm/grades1-3-national-standards-curriculum/

  https://pep.moey.gov.jm/grades-4-6-national-standards-curriculum/

  https://pep.moey.gov.jm/grade-7-9-national-standards-curriculum/

- Lambert, C. (2019, September 5). *Is there an elephant in the room? Race, colour and our national heritage.*

Jamaica Observer. http://www.jamaicaobserver.com/opinion/is-there-an-elephant-in-the-room-race-colour-and-our-african-heritage_173686?profile=1097

References

Afrobella. (2009, August 17). *Remembering old Marcus Garvey*. http://www.afrobella.com/2009/08/17/remembering-old-marcus-garvey/

Bobo Ashanti. (2020, October 17). In *Wikipedia*. https://en.wikipedia.org/wiki/Bobo_Ashanti

Boutte, G., Johnson, G., & Muki, A (2018). Revitalization of Indigenous African knowledges among people in the African diaspora. In L. Johnson, G. Boutte, G. Greene, & D. Smith (Eds.), *African diaspora literacy, the heart of transformation in K-12 schools and teacher education* (pp. 13-42). Lexington Books.

Boutte, G., Johnson, G, Wynter-Hoyte, K., & Uyota, K. E. (2017). Using African diaspora literacy to heal and restore the souls of young black children. *International Critical Childhood Studies, 6*(1), 66-79. https://journals.sfu.ca/iccps/index.php/childhoods/article/viewFile/56/pdf

Brown, D. L. (2020, August 19). *Kamala Harris's dad was from Jamaica, where a fierce woman warrior once fought slavery*. The Washington Post. https://www.washingtonpost.com/history/2020/08/19/nanny-maroons-kamala-slavery-jamaica/

Bryan, B. (2010). *Between two grammars: Research and practice for language learning and teaching in a Creole-speaking environment*. Ian Randle Publishers.

Cooper, C. (2009). Pedestrian crosses: Sites of dislocation in "post-colonial" Jamaica. *Inter-Asia Cultural Studies, 10*(1), 3-11.

Diptee, A. (2010). *From Africa to Jamaica: The making of an Atlantic slave society, 1775-1807*. University Press of Florida. http://search.ebscohost.com.libproxy.nau.edu/login.aspx?direct= true&db=nlebk&AN=482942&site=ehost-live

Twi. (2020, October 25). In *Wikipedia*. https://en.wikipedia.org/wiki/Twi#
:~:text=Twi%20(Akan%3A%20%5Bt%C9%95%E1%B6%A3i%5D,
major%20ethnic%20groups%20in%20Ghana

Williams, P. H. (2019, December 26). *Liberty Hall hosts pre-Kwanzaa fest*. The
Gleaner. http://jamaica-gleaner.com/article/news/20191226/liberty-
hall-hosts-pre-kwanzaa-fest

10

Asangha Muki, Samuel Ntewusu, Moepeola Omoegun, and Berte Van Wyk

Lessons From Africa

This chapter focuses on Africa and what we can learn to promote and advance the love of people of African descent worldwide. Promoting African diaspora people's return to the continent is not a new idea. The early 20th century saw the rise of pan-African activist Marcus Garvey's "Back to Africa" movement, which sought greater Black social and economic independence. In recent years, many Black people have traveled to Africa to visit or have relocated there. The global recognition of the need to embrace Black people's humanity and collective destiny can be seen in many ways:

- The Black Lives Matter movement https://blacklives matter.com/

- The United Nations' declaration of 2015–2024 as the International Decade for People of African Descent (Resolution 68/237) cites the need to strengthen national, regional, and international cooperation in relation to the full enjoyment of economic, social, cultural, civil, and political rights of people of African descent, and their full and equal participation in all aspects of society (United Nations, n.d.).

- In 2003, the African Union designated people of African origin who live outside the continent as Africa's Sixth Region (see Figure 10.1).

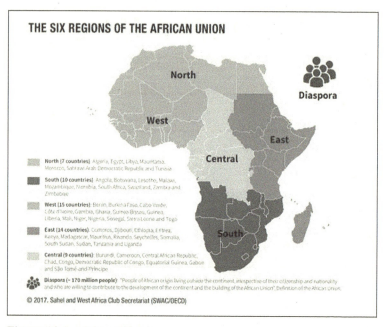

Figure 10.1. African Union
Source: Used with permission. https://stateofafricandiaspora.international/the-6th-region/.

This chapter explores lessons from three different African regions that can enhance the understanding of Africa's rich cultural heritage and showcase the continent as a beloved place not only to learn about but also to learn *from*. The first part of the chapter, by Asangha Muki, a native Cameroonian, brings an African perspective on "teaching children to be resilient, independent, and smart" focused on lessons from Cameroon in Central Africa. The second section of the chapter by Moepeola Omoegun, an indigene of Nigeria, discusses "African Indigenous and traditional education systems," focusing on lessons from Nigeria in West Africa. The third segment, by Samuel Ntewusu, includes lessons from Ghana, also in West Africa, focused on "teaching children about values using Adinkra symbols." The closing section by Berte Van Wyk from South Africa emphasizes "Indigenous Khoikhoi and San ways of knowing."

Lessons From Cameroon: Teaching Children to Be Resilient, Independent, and Smart

African instruction seeks to prepare students for adulthood. Indigenous pedagogies permit toddlers and youngsters to learn in participatory processes in the home, community, religious service, peer groups, and so forth through "work-play" activities, with little to no explicit instructional support (Nsamenang, 2008). "Child work" is a basic African cultural mode of preparing the next generation, and it is understood by both the family and the young as necessary for the family and for the youngsters' developmental learning. With Africa's traditions of "child work," children do tasks, even difficult ones, on their own.

In Cameroon, most children's "work" is undertaken in child-to-child sociability and with peer mentorship instead of with parents, other adults, or teachers. Peer cultures offer children opportunities to play, work, and learn together, free from parental supervision and adult control. Accordingly, the freedom of the peer culture breeds creativity and challenges children to cultivate prosocial values and altruism, defer to elders and more competent peers, address and resolve conflicts, and take the perspective to notice needs and serve them (Asangha, 2015; Nsamenang, 2002).

According to Fomba (2011), participatory teaching in Bali Nyonga, Cameroon, prepares youth for preparation in the labor market. Children are engaged in sustainable livelihood activities such as farming, carpentry, mechanics, craft, fishing, animal rearing, blacksmithing, and small businesses such as trading. Investment in life skills through traditional preparation strategies has been drawn from the firm belief that young people are agents of change with the potential of taking a leading role in the socioeconomic development of their communities as they transition from childhood to the world of work.

Likewise, according to Tchombe (2011), the Bamiléké child engages very early in various forms of interaction with persons and with available rich, meaningful physical and material resources. In some instances, adolescents are already the owners of a farm or a small business and a member of a "thrift and loan" or Njangi group, which is an avenue to raise capital through loans to start or sustain an existing business. Such meaningful, sustainable, and transferable experiences are fostered by inculcating the values of endurance, patience, persistence, honesty, respect, and hard work, which are indelible characteristics of the Bamiléké people of Cameroon. Perseverance, according to the people, is the key to success. In this culture, socio-affective development is the basis for developing the spirit of being socially competent (an important strand of resilient identity). These abilities, skills, and values are learned through farming and trading, the people's main economic activities. As they develop, children participate in economic activities depending on the nature and difficulty level of such tasks as selling, bargaining, and negotiating the prices of commercial wares.

What Can Black People Learn From Cameroonian Socialization of Children?

- Children are active participants in the socialization and learning process rather than just being passive recipients of adults' knowledge.

- Beginning with birth, children learn from and with parents, teachers, and adult community members.

Lessons From Nigeria: African Indigenous and Traditional Education Systems

Before British colonization, the African Indigenous system taught students practical skills to function successfully in traditional society. Usually, children 2 or 3 years of age belonged to an age group. Together, they learned the community's customs and were assigned specific duties around the village, such as sweeping lanes or clearing bush. As the children grew older, the boys were introduced to farming and more specialized work, such as wood carving or drumming. Girls would learn farming and domestic skills while boys would often enter into apprenticeship-type relations with master craftsmen. Even in the 21st century, this kind of education is expected. Examples of this can be seen in the children's book *One Big Family: Sharing Life in an African Village* (Onyefulu, 1999).

African Indigenous education is defined by Enueme (2006) as the traditional method, through which a society passes on its culture or way of life to its young ones and succeeding generations without any interference from other cultures. It is the original African way of transmitting the values and skills in a society without foreign influence at any stage or time to the young ones. Such African Indigenous education was highly advanced and included storytelling, folklores, mythologies, proverbs, songs, dance, and many other traditions (Omoegun, 2004).

In the traditional African setting, children are well valued and show each family's economic strength—especially in Nigeria. The birth of a child is usually celebrated, and names are given to highlight the significance of the child's birth. For example, there is a saying in Yoruba: *Olomo lo laiye*, meaning "those who have children have life." Names are given also to emphasize the religious faith and background of the family, such as "Ogunyemi," representing the god of iron that has beautified my life.

The newborn grew in a warm and loving environment right from birth, nurtured by the parents who provide home training, the first form of education. Such home training includes the cultural belief that everybody in the community has a say about the child's development. It is a collective responsibility to put the child on the right path and correct any misbehavior without asking for the parents' permission or consent.

In Nigeria, especially among the Southwest Yoruba-speaking group, storytelling used to be an avenue through which morals and societal values are taught from childhood to young adulthood. Such stories were usually narrated by the adults who were regarded as the residue of knowledge through their various life experiences. Children looked forward to the evenings when they would gather together to listen to "the tales by moonlight" in their various compounds.

What Can Black People Learn From Nigerian Education and Socialization?

- Children's names should be meaningful.

- We can teach values through storytelling, proverbs, and everyday activities.

- It is essential to respect elders, even if they are not blood relatives. Even today, children show respect for adults by addressing them as "auntie" and "uncle."

Lessons From Ghana: Teaching Children About Values Using Adinkra Symbols

Symbols stand for something visible. A symbol can be an object, a mark, a sign, or an abstract idea. When a child is born in Ghana, society begins to share its values with them through teaching, learning, and practice. Children are socialized into understanding society and the environment through symbols such as Adinkra symbols, which are traditional images in Ghana that are translations of thoughts and ideas in society. Adinkra is said to have originated from the name of a powerful African king in present-day Cote d'Ivoire. He was called Kofi Adinkra. In the 1800s, the Ashanti of Ghana incorporated Adinkra's art into their kingdom (Agbo, 2006). Two examples of the Adinkra symbols and their importance to children and society are discussed below.

The *Sankofa* symbol (Figure 10.2) is a bird whose body is facing forward with the head and neck looking backward. The symbol is as old as the existence of Black people. In the tombs and walls of ancient Kemet in present-day Egypt, a version of the Sankofa symbol can be found. It explains the human experience. As we go forward to the future, we also need to draw on lessons from the past. As we grow up, we do not need to abandon our ancestors' cultural traditions and values. As we face modernity, these values are also crucial in our lives since they can guide us.

Elders in Ghana often include references to Sankofa to let the children know about it and its importance. It is appropriate for an adult to tell a child, "You have made a mistake by doing A or B." The elder will conclude in Akan, "Sankofa yen Chi" (If you go back for it, it is not a taboo). The essence is to tell the child not to repeat that mistake the next time or to go back and do the right thing. Artists and members of the community also teach children to produce some of the Adinkra symbols as a pastime. The ability to make the symbols usually on calabashes, cloth, or just even painting or drawing them on objects enables the children to have a permanent register of the symbol's meanings and importance.

Figure 10.2. Sankofa Adinkra symbol, which means "go back for it"
Source: http://www.adinkra.org/htmls/adinkra/sank.htm

The *funtunfunefu* (*fu-ntu-nfu-nafu*; Figure 10.3) symbol is two Siamese crocodiles. The symbol defines the relevance of different views in society. The message conveys to children that they can express divergent views, but they are also reminded that such views must be geared toward building consensus in the end—for the betterment of society. The symbol also teaches children about the unity of purposes and the strength in unity. For example, the conjoined crocodiles have one stomach. So even though they feed separately, the food goes into one stomach. In Ghana, the symbols teach children in the community to understand that while they are individuals, they also need to work toward the community's collective good.

Figure 10.3. Funtunfunefu-denkyemfunefu (Siamese crocodiles)—a symbol of democracy and unity. "The Siamese crocodiles share one stomach, yet they fight over food." This popular symbol is a reminder that infighting and tribalism are harmful to all who engage in it.
Source: http://www.adinkra.org/htmls/adinkra/funt.htm

Usually, when a community member requests support on his farm, the elderly people take the children along. The reason is to let the children understand the way society works—especially on issues that demand collective intervention.

Right from the beginning, the children see themselves first as community members before seeing themselves as individuals. The funtunfunefu symbol also helps children appreciate from the very onset the way and manner democratic systems work, especially in their ability to debate or express their views and how such debates can lead to achieving a common objective.

Lessons From the Symbols to Black People Worldwide

Sankofa reminds Black people to hold on to their values and go back to their cultural practices that have proven to be very important for their survival and relevance. Funtufunafu tells Black people that diversity is not an excuse for disunity. Whether we find ourselves in Africa, North and South America, or the Caribbean, we come from "one stomach," born of the same color and facing the same problems—marginalization. We must therefore harness our diverse skills to achieve unity and progress.

Lessons from South Africa: Indigenous Khoikhoi and San Ways of Knowing

The Khoikhoi and San people of South Africa have always been known for their strong understandings and ways of living. Indeed, the Dutch and English were well aware of the great strength that existed among Khoikhoi and San people. For example, Lord Macaulay, in his address to the British Parliament on February 2, 1835, commented,

> I have traveled across the length and breadth of Africa and have not seen one person who is a beggar, who is a thief such wealth I have seen in the country [South Africa], such high morals values, people of such caliber, that I do not think we would ever conquer this country unless we break the very backbone of this nation, which is her spiritual; and cultural heritage and therefore, I propose that we replace

her old and ancient education system, her culture, for if the Africans think that all that is foreign and English is good and greater than their own, they will lose their self-esteem, their native culture and they will become what we want them, a truly dominate nation. (Mogoeng, 2017, p. 4)

Like other African countries, when the Dutch and English "colonized" South Africa, they suppressed our Indigenous languages. English not only became one of the media of instruction but also the dominant one (the other being Afrikaans) up till today, and Indigenous cultures had to be learned in foreign-language classes. My own experience is that I grew up in a rural area where I heard a lot of communication in my Indigenous language, but that language was suppressed by the apartheid government.

While Indigenous Khoikhoi and San languages have never been recognized as official languages, they are constitutionally recognized. The current constitution recognizes the historically diminished use and status of the Indigenous languages of our people and acknowledges that the state must take tactical and positive measures to elevate the status and advance the use of these languages.

On a positive note, local communities started to revive Indigenous languages over the last 26 years that are now formally taught in some South African schools. As a result, new books are being produced in these languages. We recognize that language development continues to be closely intertwined with and inseparable from cultural identities (Cele, 2004, p. 42). Finally, language is not just language but is related to people's emotional and identity-construction.

What Can Be Learned From Khoikhoi and San People?

African people all over the world can gain insights from Khoikhoi and San people. Three lessons include the following:

- African people must recognize and reclaim their Indigenous cultural strengths.

- We should learn and use our Indigenous languages.

- We must be careful not to let European ways dominate our ways of being and understanding.

All three of these insights are important if we are to heal ourselves as African people.

Conclusion

These lessons from Africa are important for Black people wherever we are—on the continent and in the diaspora. African traditional practices of assigning social responsibility to young people from an early age, based on African Indigenous knowledge systems, remain relevant for contemporary education goals in Africa and elsewhere. At best, this practice can serve as a context for learning about arts, values, health, and nutrition; fostering the importance of cooperation and nurturing support of others; and contributing to peaceful coexistence in society.

In many African societies, children's participation in family work is vital for developing social responsibility—an important dimension of intelligence. Work and play are better understood as complementary dimensions of activity than as separate activities. Cooperation with peers can be mobilized as a resource for co-constructive learning. Strategic opportunities for countering systemic bias in educational systems include focusing on African knowledges and languages in the curriculum and instruction.

References

Agbo, H. A. (2006). *Values of Adinkra and Agama symbols*. Bigshy Designs.

Asangha, M. N. (2015). Peer group activities and resilient identity among mid adolescents (15-17 years old): Case of Mbengwi sub division. *The African Journal of Special Education, 3*(1), 157-164.

Cele, N. (2004). 'Equity and diversity' and 'equity outcomes' challenged by language policy, politics and practice in South African higher education: The myth of language equality in education. *South African Journal of Higher Education, 18*(1), 38-56.

Enueme, C. P. (2006). *Education in Nigeria: A historical perspective.* Chambers Communication Ventures.

Fomba, (2011). Community role/engagement in vocational competence development. In A. B. Nsamenang & M. T. Tchombe, (Eds.), *Handbook of African educational theories and practices: A generative teacher education curriculum* (pp. 518-528). HDRC.

Mogoeng, M. (2017, April 24). *Opening remarks at the Fourth Congress of the Conference of Constitutional Jurisdictions of Africa (CCJA).* Cape Town, South Africa.

Nsamenang, A. B. (2002). Adolescence in sub-Saharan Africa: An image constructed from Africa's triple inheritance. In B. B. Brown, R. W. Larson, & T. S. Saraswathi (Eds.), *The world's youth: Adolescence in eight regions of the globe* (pp. 61-104). Cambridge University Press.

Nsamenang, A. B. (2008). Agency in early childhood learning and development in Cameroon. *Contemporary Issues in Early Childhood Development, 9*(3), 211-223.

Omoegun, O. M. (2004): *My story book in values for the Nigerian child.* Nigeria. Literamed Publications.

Onyefulu, I. (1999). *One big family: Sharing life in an African village.* Gardners Press.

Tchombe, T. M. (2011). Cultural strategies for cognitive enrichment in learning among the Bamiléké of west region of Cameroon. In A. B. Nsamenang & M. T. Tchombe (Eds.), *Handbook of African educational theories and practices: A generative teacher education curriculum* (pp. 205-216). HDRC.

United Nations. (n.d.). *International decade for people of African descent.* https://www.un.org/en/observances/decade-people-african-descent

11

LaGarrett J. King, Gloria Swindler Boutte,
Joyce E. King, and George L. Johnson, Jr.

Resources

Throughout the book, authors have provided resources that affirm Black culture and identity. As we conclude, we provide additional resources that will help develop culturally relevant and sustaining education for Black children.

Our first recommended resource is HomeTeam History. Hometeam History was created to advance historical perspectives concerning African history, culture, and worldview. Hometeam History has a YouTube page of African-centered animated videos for school-aged children. The videos help students learn and relearn about African people's humanity and agency.

- YouTube page: https://www.youtube.com/channel/UC121U5ymIvSpgl8KntDQUQA

Other YouTube pages about Africa:

- Africa Travel Channel: https://www.youtube.com/user/Africatravelchannel/videos

- Afrofoodtv: https://www.youtube.com/user/Afro FoodTV/videos

- The Africa Channel: https://www.youtube.com/c/theafricachanneltv/videos

Our second recommendation consists of African studies programs housed at several universities and the Association for the Study of the Worldwide African Diaspora. Both offer internet resources and teaching tips for teachers and parents.

- The University of Pennsylvania's Arts and Sciences K-12 Internet Resources on Africa: http://www.africa.upenn.edu/outreach/k-12

- African Studies Center through the Boston University Pardee School of the Global Studies department: http://www.bu.edu/africa/outreach/teachingresources/

- African Studies Program, University of Wisconsin: https://africa.wisc.edu/0-outreach-and-resources-home/2-resources/2b-online-resources/

- African Studies Center, Michigan State University: https://africa.isp.msu.edu/programs/outreach/k-12-programs/

- African Studies Program, Indiana University: https://africanstudies.indiana.edu/outreach/teaching-resources/index.html

- Center for African Studies, Howard University: https://cfas.howard.edu/outreach/k-12-teaching-resources/lesson-plans

- Kansas African Studies Center, University of Kansas: http://kasc.ku.edu/lesson-plan-and-curriculum-resources

- Association for the Study of the Worldwide African Diaspora: http://aswadiaspora.org/links/

Our third recommendation includes books that explain the importance of teaching Black children about African heritage. Check Black bookstores (see the list in the following section) for copies of these books. They are also available on Amazon.com and other websites.

- Johnson, L., Boutte, G. S., Greene, G., & Smith, D. (2018). *African diaspora literacy: The heart of transformation in K-12 schools and teacher education.* Lexington Books.

- King, J. E., & Swartz, E. E. (2014). *"Re-membering" history in student and teacher learning. An Afrocentric culturally informed praxis.* Routledge.

- Caldwell, K., & Chaves, E. (2020). *Engaging the African diaspora in K-12 education.* Peter Lang.

- Lundy, B., & Negash, S. (20130. *Teaching Africa: A guide for the 21st-century classroom.* Indiana University Press.

Our fourth recommendation is the Brown Bookshelf. The Brown Bookshelf is an online resource of Black-centered children, adolescent, and young adult books. We also include a link to a list of Black bookstores recommended by *Oprah Magazine*.

- The Brown Bookshelf: United in Story: https://the brownbookshelf.com/

Other Black Bookstores

- *Oprah Magazine* list of Black bookstores: https://www. oprahmag.com/entertainment/books/a33497812/ black-owned-bookstores/

While we are providing resources, it is not an exhaustive list. There are thousands of credible resources available worldwide. Additionally, newer and more technologically advanced resources will be created after the publication of this book. However, we cannot ignore the history of poorly constructed and violent resources made about Black people around the diaspora. Therefore, we warn readers not to use resources that present Black people using deficit lenses and perspectives. Find resources that present Black history through the lens and views of African-centered Black people. These resources can come from Black authors and illustrators and primary sources that focus on Black people's voices. While resources from White allies/co-conspirators (Love, 2019) are welcomed, it is crucial to gauge how they present information about Black people. Additionally, readers are advised to select resources about how African-descended people exhibited agency and joy in the face of endemic and systemic racism (King, 2019). Finally, remember that Blackness is global, and a complete Black history program is filled with knowledge and information from the entire diaspora.

Stay well!

References

King, L. J. (Ed.). (2020). *Perspectives of Black histories in schools*. Information Age Publishing.

Love, B. L. (2019). *We want to do more than survive: Abolitionist teaching and the pursuit of educational freedom*. Beacon Press.

Appendix A:

Dimensions of African American Culture

1. **Oral tradition**—strengths in oral/aural modes of communication, in which both speaking and listening are treated as performances, and cultivation of oral virtuosity. The ability to use alliterative, metaphorically colorful, graphic forms of spoken language. This does not mean that strengths do not exist in written and other literacy traditions as well.

2. **Spirituality**—an approach to life as being essentially vitalistic rather than mechanistic, with the conviction that nonmaterial forces influence people's everyday lives

3. **Harmony**—the notion that one's fare is interrelated with other elements in the scheme of things, so that humankind and nature are harmonically conjoined

4. **Movement**—an emphasis on the interweaving of movement, rhythm, percussiveness, music, and dance, all of which are taken as central to psychological health

5. **Verve**—a propensity for relatively high levels of stimulation and for action that is energetic and lively

6. **Affect**—an emphasis on emotions and feelings, together with a specific sensitivity to emotional cues and a tendency to be emotionally expressive

7. **Communalism/collectivity**—a commitment to social connectedness, which includes an awareness that

social bonds and responsibilities transcend individual privilege

8. **Expressive individualism**—the cultivation of a distinctive personality and proclivity for spontaneous, genuine personal expression

9. **Social time perspective**—an orientation in which time is treated as passing through a social space rather than a material one, and in which time can be recurring, personal, and phenomenological

10. **Perseverance**—ability to maintain a sense of agency and strength in the face of adversities

11. **Improvisation**—substitution of alternatives that are more sensitive to Black culture. Examples can be seen in the artwork, music, language, clothing, food, and everyday culture.

Source: Boykin, 1994; Hale-Benson, 1986

 Appendix B:

Ten Principles for Black Education and Socialization

1. We exist as African People, an ethnic family. Our perspective must be centered in that reality.

2. The priority is on the African ethnic family over the individual. Because we live in a world where expertness in alien cultural traditions (that we also share) have gained hegemony, our collective survival and enhancement must be our highest priorities.

3. Some solutions to problems that involve differential use of three modes of response to domination and hegemony: Adaptation—adopting what is deemed useful; Improvisation—substituting or improvising alternatives that are more sensitive to our culture; and Resistance—resisting that which is destructive and not in the best interests of our people.

4. The "ways of knowing" provided by the arts and humanities are often more useful in informing our understanding of our lives and experiences and those of other oppressed people than the knowledge and methodologies of the sciences that have been privileged by the research establishment despite the often distorted or circumscribed knowledge and understanding this way of knowing produces.

5. Paradoxically, from the perspective of the education research establishment, knowledge production is viewed as the search for facts and (universal) truth, while the

circumstances of our social and existential condition require the search for meaning and understanding.

6. The priority is on research validity over inclusion. For research validity, highest priority must be placed on studies of:

   a) African tradition (history, culture and language);

   b) Hegemony (e.g., uses of schooling/socialization and incarceration);

   c) Equity (funding, teacher quality, content and access to technology); and

   d) Beneficial practice (at all levels of education, from childhood to elderhood).

7. Research informs practice and practice informs research in the production and utilization of knowledge; therefore, context is essential in research:

   a) cultural/historical context;

   b) political/ economic context; and

   c) professional context, including the history of AERA and African people.

8. We require power and influence over our common destiny. Rapid globalization of the economy and cyber-technology are transforming teaching, learning and work itself. Therefore, we require access to education that serves our collective interests, including assessments that address

cultural excellence and a comprehensive approach to the interrelated health, learning and economic needs of African people.

9. The Universal Declaration of Human Rights proclaims, and the UNESCO World Education 2000 Report, recently issued in Dakar, Senegal, affirms that "education is a fundamental human right" and "an indispensable means for effective participation in the societies and economies of the twenty-first century." We are morally obligated to "create safe, healthy, inclusive, and equitably resourced educational environments" conducive to excellence in learning and socialization with clearly defined levels of achievement for all. Such learning environments must include appropriate curricula and teachers who are appropriately educated and rewarded.

10. African people are not empty vessels. We are not new to the study of and practice of education and socialization that is rooted in deep thought. We will not accept a dependent status in the approach and solution to our problems.

Source: King, 2005

References

Boykin, A. W. (1994). Afrocultural expression and its implications for schooling. In E. R. Hollins, J. E. King, & W. C. Hayman (Eds.), *Teaching diverse populations: Formulating a knowledge base* (pp. 243-273). State University of New York Press.

Hale-Benson, J. E. (1986). *Black children: Their roots, culture, and learning styles (Rev. ed.).* Johns Hopkins University Press.

Hilliard, A. G. (1992). Behavioral style, culture, and teaching, and learning. *Journal of Negro Education, 61*(3), 370-377.

King, J. E. (2005). *Black education: A transformative research and action agenda for the new century.* Routledge.

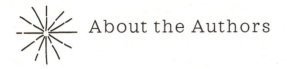

About the Authors

Janice Baines is a second-grade teacher in Columbia, South Carolina. She began her undergraduate studies at Benedict College, where she obtained a BS degree in early childhood education. She earned her MEd in curriculum and instruction from the University of Wisconsin and is a PhD student at the University of South Carolina. She is a co-author of *We've Been Doing it Your Way Long Enough: Choosing the Culturally Relevant Classroom*. Her research interests are culturally relevant and sustaining pedagogies and diaspora literacies.

Gloria Swindler Boutte is a Carolina Distinguished Professor at the University of South Carolina. Her scholarship, teaching, and service focuses on equity pedagogies. She is the author/editor of four books: (1) *African Diaspora Literacy: The Heart of Transformation in K-12 Schools and Teacher Education* (2019 AESA Critics Choice Award) (2) *Educating African American Students: And how are the children*; (3) *Resounding Voices: School Experiences of People From Diverse Ethnic Backgrounds*; and (4) *Multicultural Education: Raising Consciousness*. She has received millions of dollars in grants and has more than 90 publications. Gloria has received prestigious Fulbright Scholar and Fulbright Specialist awards and is the founder and Executive Director of the Center for the Education and Equity of African American Students (CEEAAS). She has presented and/or served as a visiting scholar internationally in every continent except Antarctica. She is the co-author (with George Johnson) of *Drs. Diaspora Curriculum*—a curriculum that teaches P-12 students about African and African American history.

Shayla Calhoun is an African American educator with more than 10 years of teaching experience. She has a Bachelor of Science in Elementary Education from the University of Southern Indiana and a Master of Arts from Oakland City University. She is currently working on obtaining a doctorate in educational leadership at the University of Southern Indiana. She brings to the table her own unique experiences along with a lifelong passion to empower students to be themselves and fully embrace it through literature.

Saudah Collins has served as a professional educator for more than 23 years and is currently a teacher for the Center for the Education and Equity of African American Students. She has focused her life and academic pursuits around issues of equity. As a National Board–certified teacher, she has taught prekindergarten through fifth grades, with a specialization in early childhood. Saudah has been selected twice as a Fulbright-Hayes participant, traveling to Cameroon and Ghana, West Africa.

Julia Dawson teaches sixth- and seventh-grade social studies at W. A. Perry Middle School in Columbia, South Carolina. She loves learning daily from W. A. Perry teenagers and their families; teachers, administrators, and staff; and local and state champions of education justice.

Jamon Dubose was born and raised in Aiken, South Carolina. He is a recent graduate of Aiken High School. He is attending college majoring in fine arts/education. Jamon is a local youth activist and leads a chapter of youth leaders called Next Generation. He frequently gives back to his community by volunteering.

Leslie K. Etienne is Visiting Professor of Africana Studies and Urban Teacher Education at Indiana University–Purdue University, Indianapolis (IUPUI). He also serves as the director of the Africana studies program. His research is focused on Black emancipatory education, the histories in the African diaspora, and leadership in the Black liberation movements, arts administration, and public history. He is also the project director for the IUPUI School of Education/ Children's Defense Fund Freedom School.

Antoinette Gibson is a veteran Social Teacher in Richland One School District. Antoinette has received several rewards: Every Black Girl's Community Leader, 1# Scores for Standardized testing in Social Studies, Best Early Bird Program in South Carolina, and WLTX Teacher of Week and recognition as a teacher for the Excellence and Equity of American Students. Antoinette has organized a boys' youth group to focus on academics and social and emotional well-being. She continues to mentor and motivate students to excel.

Valente' Gibson is a fifth-grade teacher at Jackson Creek Elementary in Columbia, South Carolina. Currently, in his role as a fifth-grade teacher, he focuses his research and teaching on racial and social justice education practices while working to promote equity in issues of race, gender, class, and sexuality. In his work, he has centered on the brilliance of Black students and their families as anti-racist pedagogy. Gibson is also a teacher for the Center for the Education and Equity of African American Students.

Kayla Hostetler is an English educator. She is the recipient of the 2019 NCTE and SCTE High School Teacher of Excellence Award. Kayla is a Center for the Education and Equity of African American Students (CEEAAS) teacher. She received the CEEAAS Center's 2018 Advocate for African American Students award. Kayla is a mentor of a youth activist group called SC Next Generation. This group focuses on leading students to identify problems in their community and take action. She has several publications focusing on teaching for social justice and raising critical consciousness.

Joy Howard is presently an assistant professor of teacher education at the University of Southern Indiana. Her work utilizes critical race frameworks to interrogate issues of race and racism in education broadly and to make sense of the educational experiences of Black mixed-race students more specifically.

Jarvais Jackson earned his undergraduate degree from Winthrop University in Elementary Education, followed by earning a Master of Education at Columbia College. He is currently pursuing a PhD in Teaching and Learning at the University of South Carolina. Focusing particularly on the educational experiences of Black people, Jarvais's research is situated in critical race theory, culturally relevant pedagogy, and BlackCrit. Jarvais has taught in elementary, middle, and undergraduate courses.

Tambra O. Jackson is the interim dean and a professor of urban teacher education at the Indiana University School of Education, Indianapolis. Her research focuses on culturally relevant/sustaining pedagogies, teachers of color, and the teacher identities and praxis of Black women educators and faculty. She resides in Indianapolis with her husband, Les, and their son, Kadir.

George L. Johnson, Jr. is Professor and Academic Program Coordinator of Special Education at South Carolina State University. For more than two decades, Dr. Johnson's scholarship, teaching and service has focused on equity pedagogies, teaching for social justice and critical race theory in education with an emphasis on culturally and linguistically diverse students. He has taught and presented nationally and internationally on special education, diversity, and disproportionality, community, and equity issues. Dr. Johnson has numerous publications and has received $300,000 in grants. He has presented his work in Nigeria, Australia, New Zealand, England, Botswana, South Africa, and Sierra Leone. He is the co-author (with Gloria Boutte) of *Drs. Diaspora Curriculum*—a curriculum that teaches P-12 students about African and African American history.

Lasana D. Kazembe is an assistant professor at Indiana University-Purdue University, Indianapolis, where he teaches in the School of Education (Department of Teacher Education, Curriculum, and Foundations) and in the Africana studies program. He is a published poet, spoken-word artist, educational consultant, and scholar of urban teacher education, global Black arts movements, and the Black radical tradition in education. His latest (edited) book, titled *Keeping Peace: Reflections on Life, Legacy, Commitment, and Struggle* (2018), was published by Third World Press Foundation.

Joyce E. King holds the Benjamin E. Mays Endowed Chair for Urban Teaching, Learning and Leadership at Georgia State University (GSU) in the Department of Educational Policy Studies. She holds affiliated faculty status in the Department of African American Studies, the Women's and Gender Studies Institute, the Partnership for Urban Health Research and the Urban Studies Institute. Her publications in the *Harvard Educational Review*, the *Journal of Negro Education*, *International Journal of Qualitative Studies in Education*, the *Journal of African American History* focus on a transformative role for culture in curriculum and urban teacher effectiveness, morally engaged, community-mediated inquiry and Black education research and policy. Her most recent book is *Heritage Knowledge in the Curriculum: Retrieving an African Episteme* (with E. Swartz). Dr. King is past president of the American Educational Research Association, President of the Board of Directors of the Institute for Food and Development Policy (FoodFirst.org), a member of the National African American Reparations Commission and a recipient of the Stanford University School of Education Alumni Excellence Award (2018). A recent essay, "To Create a More Perfect Union, We the People Need Reparations to Heal Our Wounded Souls," is published on the American Civil Liberties Union website https://www.aclu.org/issues/create-more-perfect-union-we-people-need-reparations-heal-our-wounded-souls.

LaGarrett J. King is a former high school teacher in Georgia and Texas. Currently, he is the Isabella Wade Lyda and Paul Lyda Professor of Education and founding director of the CARTER Center for K12 Black History Education at the University of Missouri. He is an award-winning scholar whose research focuses on the teaching and learning of Black history in schools and society.

Dr. Clement T. M. Lambert is an associate professor and chair in the Department of Teaching & Learning at Northern Arizona University. He also served in faculty and administrative positions at the at undergraduate and graduate levels in the School of Education, University of the West Indies for 20 years. His research and publications are primarily in literacy education and includes violence prevention in schools and teacher education curriculum change.

Shaquetta Moultrie is a middle-level social studies teacher. She has scored number one in standardized testing for

African American males. She was honored as law educator of the year for the South Carolina Bar association for her work with middle-level mock trial students.

Meir Muller has rabbinical ordination as well as a doctorate in the area of early childhood education. Dr. Muller serves as an assistant professor in the College of Education at the University of South Carolina. His research interests include anti-racist pedagogy, and teacher preparation. Dr. Muller is part of a team developing curricula that prepare European teachers to counter bias, prejudice, and anti-Semitism. Dr. Muller is also in his 29th year with the Cutler Jewish Day School, a school for children birth through the fifth grade.

Kindel Nash is an associate professor of early childhood education at the University of Maryland Baltimore County. Her work focuses on fostering equity and justice in teaching through fore-fronting the early literacy practices of high performing teachers in urban public school contexts.

Ricardo Neal is the founder and chief executive officer of We Will All Rise. He has served in various leadership and governance roles for 25 years within education, philanthropy, and public advocacy and has led community change work nationally and internationally. He earned a bachelor's degree in political science from the University of Massachusetts Amherst and a master's degree in social work from the Boston University School of Social Work. Born in St. Catherine, Jamaica, and raised in Lawrence, Massachusetts, Ricardo currently lives in Baltimore, Maryland, with his wife and two children.

Asangha Muki is a university lecturer of psychology and a researcher. He is affiliated to the Centre for Research on Child and Family Development and Education, Limbe, Cameroon; Cameroon Psychology Association; the International Society for the Study of Behavioural Development; and the International Association of Cross Cultural Psychology, and he is an affiliate faculty member at Centre for the Education and Equity of African American Students at University of South Carolina, Columbia.

Samuel Ntewusu has worked as research fellow at the Institute of African Studies, University of Ghana. He teaches Chieftaincy and Development in Africa (undergraduate course) and, in collaboration with other lecturers, handles the following postgraduate courses: The Slave Trade and Africa, African Historiography and Methodology, Colonial Rule and African Responses, and Pan Africanism. He has supervised a number of graduate students in their research projects/theses both in and outside of Ghana.

Moepeola Omoegun is a Professor of Guidance and Counseling at the University of Lagos (UNILAG), Nigeria. She served as a former Dean of the Faculty of Education UNILAG and Pioneer Dean of Education for Ajayi Crowther University, Oyo. She is also a member of the Governing Council of Ajayi Crowther University, Oyo.

Berte Van Wyk is a former chairperson of the Caribbean and African Studies in Education Special Interest Group at the American Educational Research Association. He is the current president of the African Development and Education Research Association. He is also a former chairperson of the Department of Education Policy Studies at Stellenbosch University in South Africa. His research focuses on institutional culture, Indigenous Khoikhoi and San epistemologies, and philosophy of higher education.

Kamania Wynter-Hoyte is an assistant professor in the Instruction and Teacher Education Department at the University of South Carolina. Her research interests are culturally relevant and sustaining pedagogy, African diaspora literacy, and community literacy practices. Kamania's work has been published in the *International Critical Childhood Policy Studies Journal, Equity & Excellence in Education,* the *International Journal of Qualitative Studies in Education, Race Ethnicity and Education,* and *Journal of Negro Education.*

Index